Scottish Words

A Very Peculiar History™

A wee splore o Scots

(A little celebration of the Scots language)

With thanks to Mary,
my very kind neighbour

DA

Editor: Stephen Haynes

Artist: David Lyttleton

Published in Great Britain in MMXIII by
Book House, an imprint of
The Salariya Book Company Ltd
25 Marlborough Place, Brighton BN1 1UB
www.salariya.com

ISBN: 978-1-908759-63-4

SCRIBO   BOOK HOUSE   SCRIBBLERS

3 5 7 9 8 6 4

A CIP catalogue record for this book is available
from the British Library.

Printed and bound in China.
Printed on paper from sustainable sources.
Reprinted in MMXVIII.

Visit
www.salariya.com
for our online catalogue and
free fun stuff.

Scottish Words
A Very Peculiar History™

Written by
Fiona Macdonald

Created and designed by
David Salariya

BOOK HOUSE
a SALARIYA imprint

Guid things come in
sma' bulk.

Scots proverb

Contents

"

Scots is one of the
pleasures of living in
Scotland, with its rich
vocabulary, its smeddum
and virr…

Paul Scott, quoted in *The Scotsman*, 2009

smeddum: spirit; virr: energy.

"

INTRODUCTION

What would you say if someone gave you a *bap*, a *dap*, or a *garron*? How would you feel if they called you a *dux* or a *sneuter*? Do you know what to do with a *flane*, a *hushock*, a *kist*, or a *tassie*? Could you wear *raploch* or *schort-hoozle*? Eat a cake that was *gibbery*, or *kneggum*? And, with your nearest and dearest, how would you fancy a spot of *houghmagandie*?

North of the Border, it's not just the accent that's different, the whole *language* is not the same.

Words and meanings

Here's an explanation of the Scots words used above:

bap soft, flat bread roll, usually dusted with flour

dap gym shoe

garron small, sturdy horse

dux top student

sneuter slow, stupid person

flane arrow

hushock heap

kist box or storage chest

tassie cup

raploch old name for coarse homespun cloth

schort-hoozle old name for shorts or knee breeches

gibbery gingery

kneggum foul-smelling

houghmagandie cuddles, kisses (and more)

Ways of speaking

In fact, there are three main languages in Scotland. Gaelic is known, and promoted, in the Highlands and Islands; English is spoken everywhere. Visitors and settlers have brought their own ways of speaking with them – from the 'refined' southern British speech of wealthy huntin', shootin', fishin' estate-owners, to languages with their own diverse heritage, such as Italian, Polish, Yiddish, Urdu and Bengali. In the 20th century, mass media introduced words from Hollywood, rock'n'roll and TV; in the 21st, txt-speak and the latest social media verbal codes have, among other things, increased the communication gap between generations.

But this book will focus on Scots – the language of the majority of Scottish people for the past thousand years and more. Scots has also travelled: first to Northern Ireland from about 1600, and, later, right round the world. How many people in (for example) America, Canada, Australia or Hong Kong do not recognise *scone* or *stymie*, *lass* or *loony* – or (of course) *kilt* and *golf*? *Gump* (as in Forrest

Gump) is a good Scots word; so are *hassle*, and *bonnie*, and *porridge*. Even *slogan* is Scots, although it originally meant 'war-cry'.

Today, Scots words are still spreading. Experts report that favourite Scots insults such as *ned* (unruly youth) and *mingin* (revolting) are filling a vocabulary gap on the streets of London. However, some of the best Scots words of disapproval – *crabbit*, *nippet* (bad-tempered), *clype* (tell-tale), *numpty* (fool), *carnaptious* (quarrelsome) and *ramgunshoch* (utterly boorish) – have stayed safely at home.

For almost 300 years, enthusiasts for the Scots language have worried about its decline, and prophesied its disappearance (see page 60). But Scots still survives and flourishes – everywhere from school playgrounds to elegant poetry pages, and also in the Scottish Parliament. Today, the estimated number of regular Scots speakers is somewhere between 1.5 and 2.5 million, out of a total Scottish population of around 5.2 million (2010 figures). Many more Scottish residents (about 85 per cent, according to the Scottish Government in 2010) mingle English and

Scots words together, depending on their mood, the people they are with, or the place they find themselves in. They find Scots words apt, and useful. As Carl MacDougall, a champion of the Scots language, has pointed out, many Scots words cannot be neatly translated. They express a thought, feeling or description with particular precision and power. Consider, for example, *eerie*, or *wersh*, or *scunner*. There are many more.

Words of our own

Scotland is not a large country, but it finds room to house a surprising number of regional Scots dialects, from Borders in the south to Patter in Glasgow, Doric and Dundonian in the east and Orcadian in the far northern isles. Often unintelligible to outsiders, these local ways of speaking have nothing to do with the Scottish accent – although that varies greatly, as well. Instead, they have their own local words, phrases, spellings and even grammar. Scots dialects reflect the history, landscape, occupations and interests of the people who lived – and still live – in all the different Scottish regions.

Pollsters puggled

puggled: exhausted; at the end of one's resources

Nobody knows precisely how many Scots speakers live in Scotland today – not even the skilled pollsters who tested questions for the Scottish Census in 2011. (That was the first time that a query about the Scots language appeared on the census form.) Why this ignorance? Because Scottish men and women, even guid, braid Scots speakers, sometimes seem not to know themselves. In 2009, the testers discovered that:

* Some Scots think that Scots is slang, not a proper language.

* Some Scots think that it's just a dialect or variety of English.

* Some Scots think that 'Scots' means any words spoken with a Scottish accent.

* Some Scots say that Scots is old and dead, or just for poetry.

* Some Scots don't know that the words they use every day are uniquely Scottish.

* Some Scots fear that admitting to speaking Scots might make them look stupid or ignorant.

* A few Scots think that 'Scots' means Gaelic.

Pity the poor pollsters! Faced with such a *boorach* (muddle), they were forced to admit defeat:

> The number of Scots speakers will either be overestimated or underestimated…The question will not yield any meaningful data on Scots….We cannot see any way to solve this problem in the context of the Census.
>
> http://www.gro-scotland.gov.uk/files2/the-census/ preparations/2011-census-language-question.pdf

What a whigmaleerie!

whigmaleerie: fantastical or extraordinary thing.

Playing politics

To be fair, some of these misconceptions by Scots about Scots seem to be shared by people who perhaps should know better – and for other-than-linguistic reasons. In 2010, a Conservative MSP (Member of the Scottish Parliament) declared:

> The Scots language that the SNP [Scottish National Party] government continues to try to promote is not a separate language, but a collection of regional dialects of the English language... The SNP must stop wasting taxpayers' money trying to invent something that does not exist, in a futile attempt to promote the narrow Nationalist agenda.

Dear Readers, unlike the speaker quoted above, the author of this book is not political point-scoring. But, in the eyes of many – most – scholars, that MSP was simply wrong. Scots *is* a language – and (for what it's worth) has been officially recognised as such by the European Community. In 2001, Scots was classified as a 'regional or minority language' by European Charter, and this decision was accepted by the British Government later the same year.

Peculiarly, although Scots has no similar official status within Scotland itself, it *is* formally recognised as a 'traditional language' in Northern Ireland. That classification was made by The North/South Co-Operation (Implementation Bodies) Northern Ireland Order, in 1999.

Today, anyone, Scots or not, wishing to discover whether they are a Scots speaker can consult a self-check website (yes, really: it's at http://www.ayecan.com/). Or they can read, listen to, watch and enjoy the thousands of recent Scottish books, poems, songs, plays and films that feature Scots words and sayings. They can learn Scots at evening classes or online, and even buy a speak-along CD to help them practise the perfect Scottish accent. Best of all, they can walk along Scottish streets, ride on Scottish buses and trains, hunt for bargains in Scottish shops, listen to Scottish people speaking – and join in.

They can also, of course, find out more about the splendid Scots language and its speakers from this little book. Read on, and enjoy. *Here's tae ye all!*

"

Does not 'humdudgeon' evoke a pointless outcry better than any English equivalent? Is not 'mixter-maxter' hugely superior to 'jumble'? Does not 'beflum' outclass 'befool' or 'cajole'?

The Guardian, Friday 18 January 2008

"

CHAPTER ONE

PAST AND PRESENT

Scots is often called a traditional language, and sometimes sounds as if it must be very ancient indeed. Try saying these words out loud, for example: *bairn* (child); *thole* (suffer), *schonk* (shatter), *thrawn* (twisted or contrary), *muck* (muck!) and *wersslete* (hunting dog). What images do they conjure up? Perhaps a family of primitive hunters, shivering in the Scottish winter, armed with stone tools and nets of roughly twisted bark, leading a life that was not only mucky and muddy, but also nasty, brutish and short?

That image perhaps sounds convincing, but in fact, compared with many other European languages, Scots is a mere youngster. The language that eventually developed into Scots arrived in southern Scotland some time between AD 600 and 700. Where did it come from, and what was its name?

At an Angle...

To some Scots the news may be shocking, but their 'traditional tongue' came from south of the Border, and, before that, from across the North Sea. Linguists identify Scots as a Germanic language. It developed from the speech of the Angles, warriors and perhaps farmers who came to the British Isles from Denmark and took control of the kingdom of Bernicia (based in modern Northumberland and nearby). Known as Anglo-Saxon or Old English, their language was also the ancestor of the modern English spoken all round the world today.

Scots contains several Anglo-Saxon words that have disappeared from everyday English, such as *bannock* (flat cake), *haugh* (wood) and *ben* (inside). There is also *weird*, which, south of the Border, has – weirdly? – changed its meaning, though its original sense survives in Scots: *We maun ðree our weirð* (We must endure our fate).

Hame sweet hame?

We do not know how many Danish Angles arrived to live in Scotland, although recent genetic research suggests that it may not have been very many. That need not have mattered; if they were powerful enough, their language would have spread, by imitation and through dealings with weaker local peoples.

In Scotland, we can discover where Old English was spoken from the names that the speakers gave to their settlements. More than any other nouns, place names remain the same over the centuries. Many towns, villages and farms in south and southeast Scotland, and a smaller number in Ayrshire, still have Old English names.

Sassenach (Saxon) speak

Some Anglo-Saxon place names in Scotland:

Auldehame *ald* (old) and *hame* (farm)

Ayton *ea* (water) and *tun* (settlement)

Earlsferry *earl* (nobleman) and *feri* (river crossing)

Kelso *calc* (chalk) and *how* (hill)

Motherwell *modor* (mother, Virgin Mary) and *well* (spring or well)

Polwarth *pol* (pool) and *worth* (enclosure)

Prestwick *priest* and *wic* (farm)

Roxburgh Hroc's (a man's name, meaning 'Rook') and *burgh* (settlement)

Wark castle, fort

Life before English

But people had been living in Scotland for at least 8,000 years before the first speakers of Old English reached Scottish shores. How did they communicate? Before around 1000 BC (or, some scholars say, 3000 BC), our imaginary prehistoric Scottish family on page 17 would have spoken an unknown tongue, which may or may not have been an ancestor of one of today's Indo-European languages. Genetic evidence suggests that many of today's Scots are descended from people who arrived there after the last Ice Age from northwest Spain. But if our imaginary family lived after around 1000 BC, they would almost certainly have spoken Pictish, the first named Scottish language that we know about.

Pictish, the language of the *Pechts* ('the people'), was a Celtic language. It is now extinct, but was closely related to Welsh. At the time Old English arrived, Pictish was spoken in many regions of Scotland, especially the north and east. A very similar Celtic language, Brythonic, was spoken in the southwest Scottish kingdom of Strathclyde.

The Picts (and Britons) were here! And here! And here!

Although there are no written records of the Pictish language, hundreds of Pictish and Brythonic words survive in Scottish place names:

Aberdeen *aber* (place where rivers join) and Don (river name)

Alvie *al* (rocky)

Arran *aran* (peaked hill)

Cardross *cardden* (wooded) mixed with Gaelic *ross* (headland)

Fochabers *fothach* (lake) and *aber* (place where rivers join)

Glasgow *glas* (green) and *cau* (hollow)

Penicuik *pen* (hill), *y* (the) and *cog* (cuckoo)

Pitlochry *pit* (piece, or share, of land) mixed with later (Gaelic) word *cloichreach* (stones)

Restenneth *ros* (moor) and *tened* (of fire)

Stones and symbols

Until very recently, no traces had ever been found of Pictish writing. But on 31 March 2010, the following exciting article appeared on the Discovery News website:

New Written Language of Ancient Scotland Discovered

Once thought to be rock art, carved depictions of soldiers, horses and other figures are in fact part of a written language dating back to the Iron Age.

Yes, readers, that's right. The Picts wrote in pictures! They placed picture-symbols on tall stones scattered across the landscape where they once lived. Hundreds of these carvings still survive. Like today's warning road-signs or instructions on how to assemble flat-pack furniture, the pictures represent units of information, not sounds or words.

The experts cannot yet decipher the code, but have a wonderful word for it: semasiography.

Minding your *ps* and *qs*

Over 2000 years ago, Celtic languages were widely spoken in Europe. Most are now extinct, but a few still survive – almost all of them in the British Isles.

Scholars sometimes divide these languages into two groups, named after key differences of pronunciation. They call Pictish, Welsh, Cornish and Breton 'p-Celtic'. Scottish and Irish Gaelic, together with Manx, are labelled 'q-Celtic'.

* In p-Celtic the word for 'son' sounds like *map* or *ap*.

* In q-Celtic the word for 'son' sounds like *maqq* or *mac*.

It's only fair to add, however, that other experts classify Celtic languages quite differently, depending on how – and how much – they have changed over time. They identify two distinct branches: Insular Celtic (all the varieties spoken in the British Isles, plus Breton, spoken in northwest France) and Continental Celtic.

Alba

However, from around AD 500, Pictish was being challenged by a rival Celtic language. Often known today as Goidelic, it was the ancestor of modern Scottish and Irish Gaelic, and was spoken by people living on both sides of the Irish Sea. As they grew more powerful, their language began to spread throughout Scotland from their strongholds on the far west Scottish coast.

By around AD 1000, Gaelic-speaking kings had taken control of the Pictish lands and created a new Scottish kingdom: Alba. They had also conquered the southern Scottish kingdoms of Strathclyde and Bernicia (Northumberland), creating, for the first time ever, a single state that ruled very nearly all of Scotland (though Orkney and Shetland belonged to Norway until annexed by Scotland in 1469). Their Gaelic language gradually replaced Pictish and Brythonic, but, in the former Bernicia and in southeast Scotland, Old English was still going (very) strong.

Land of lochs and glens

Some Gaelic place names:

Balmoral *baile* (homestead, village) and *moral*
(big, splendid)

Benbecula *beinn* (mountain), *na* (of) and *faoghail*
(salt-water ford)

Carnoustie *carraig* (rock), *na* (of) and *ghiuthais*
(fir tree)

Dundee *dun* (hill, fort) and Daig (man's name)

Glen Roy *gleann* (narrow valley), *ruaidh* (red)

Invergarry *inver* (river mouth), *garry* (rough)

Largo *leargach* (steep place)

Lochindorb *loch* (lake), *an* (of) and *doirb*
(tadpoles)

Torphichen *torr* (hill) and *phigheainn* (magpies)

Raiders from the sea

However, the Gaelic-speaking kings of Alba were not the only powers in the land. From around AD 800, bands of Vikings – pirate raiders from Scandinavia – terrorised Scottish coasts. They were followed by parties of traders and settlers. Naturally, they brought their own language (Norse, or Norn) with them. They renamed the sheltered harbours where they moored their ships, the cliffs, headlands and the other landmarks that they steered by, the bays where they built their farms and byres – and much, much, more, from wildlife to clothes, food, close relatives, and tools (they gave us *deer*, *shirt*, *egg*, *sister* and *knife*, not to mention such basic words as *they*, *them* and *their*). Many words of Norse origin still survive in Scots today.

Wiking words

Well, that's what they say in Norway. Here are some place names brought by the Norsemen:

Acharacle *ath* (ford) and Thorkill (man's name)

Biggar *bygg* (barley) and *garðr* (enclosed field)

Dingwall *thing* (council, assembly) and *vollr* (open space)

Farr passage for ships

Isbister Ine (man's name) and *bolstaðr* (farmstead)

Kismul *kistu* (glen) and *muli* (bare)

Marwick *mar* (seagull) and *vik* (sea-inlet)

Pabay *papa* (priest) and *ey* (island)

Waternish *vatr* (water) and *nes* (headland)

Saintly sayings

In AD 1070, Scottish King Malcolm III married an English princess, Margaret. She spoke Old English, could read and write, and was devoted to charity work and the Christian Church. (She was made a saint after she died.) She gave her royal children English, not Scottish, names: Edward, Edmund, Ethelred, Edgar, Alexander (OK, he's the exception – it's ancient Greek, after the Macedonian hero-warrior), David, Edith, Mary. (Mary and David are names from the Bible, and were better known in England than in Scotland).

Margaret's descendants, the Scottish kings who ruled after Malcolm, encouraged priests and monks to spread their religious message to the Scots. Most of these holy men came from northern England (Yorkshire, in particular) and, as well as Church Latin, brought their own local version of Old English with them. This contained many words introduced to northern England by Danish Vikings, such as *kirk* (church) and *gate* (street). It spread first throughout southern Scotland, and then northeastwards around the coast.

Kings, monks and barons

Margaret's son, King David I (reigned 1124–1153), and the kings who ruled after him, introduced yet one more foreign language to Scotland when they recruited Norman barons and knights to lead their armies and defend the royal family. The newcomers spoke French, which soon escaped from their fine castles to become the fashion at the Scottish royal court. Scottish kings also made many friendly contacts – later known as the 'Auld Alliance' – with French kings and princes; Scots and French shared a fear of England's warlike ambitions, and a deep mistrust of English kings. Like their saintly ancestor, Queen Margaret, Scots kings invited churchmen to settle in their country, especially monks from France.

French words that came into the Scots language at around this time include *ashet* (plate or dish), *coup* (rubbish tip), *douce* (mild, gentle) and *tassie* (cup). Later French arrivals include *fash* (bother) and, according to some authorities, *Hogmanay* (New Year).

Talking trade

Lower down the social scale, merchants, shopkeepers, builders, carpenters, blacksmiths, innkeepers, servants, soldiers, sailors, fisher-families and craftsmen and women of all kinds moved to live in the new market towns. These were built by Scottish kings and barons in the shadow of their castles or at sheltered anchorages around the coast. The townsfolk hoped for protection and the chance to buy and sell; kings and barons planned to collect tolls and taxes from trade.

Some townspeople came from Scotland; some from south of the Border. But many arrived on regular visits from nations across the North Sea: Sweden and Denmark, Poland, Germany, the Netherlands and what is now Belgium. Scots also migrated to mainland Europe to work as traders or in the fishing industry, setting up 'Scottish quarters' in many busy ports. Rough, tough Scottish mercenary soldiers – known by the splendid Scots name of *gallowglasses* (from Gaelic *galloglaigh* 'young foreign warrior') – served in the armies of many European kings.

Origins of words spoken in non-Gaelic areas of
Scotland c.1400 (all figures very approximate):

Old English	66%
Norse	12%
French	9%
Latin	5%
Dutch/German	2%
Celtic	2%
Other/unknown	4% (proper names, onomatopoeic, etc.)

These figures (based on http://www.dsl.ac.uk/)
exclude place names, which were – and are –
overwhelmingly Celtic.

All these North Sea travellers and traders
brought new words to Scotland. *Croon* (sing
softly), *pinkie* (little finger), *scone* – and *gowf*
(golf) – are all from Dutch. This last import
suggests that Scotland's most famous game is
perhaps not local in origin. Some people may
find this a worry.

By around 1300, people living in Scotland had
a wide variety of words to choose from.

Except in the Highlands and Western Islands, where everyone still spoke Gaelic, most Scots people found themselves talking in a language based on Old English, but liberally scattered with words from Pictish, Gaelic, Norse, French, Latin, German and Dutch. Just a few were beginning to write in Scots, too – but that's the topic for our next chapter.

Scots or what?

What did Scottish people call this new language? Logically, but confusingly, 'Inglis'. To compound the confusion, unless they were Gaelic speakers, they also often called Gaelic 'Scots'. And educated people, writing in Latin, sometimes called any kind of Inglis 'German'.

However, the 'Inglis' spoken in Scotland was becoming increasingly different from the 'Middle English' used south of the Border. The gap between the two was widened by long years of war between the English and the Scots. In Scotland, 'Inglis' speakers followed the style set in Scotland's capital, Edinburgh. In England, the soft southern speech of London and the southeast became the ideal.

Look out! Vowels shifting about!

In the years between around AD 1350 and 1500, there was a major change in the way that southern English was spoken. Some vowel sounds were 'raised' (pronounced with the tongue higher up in the mouth), while others became diphthongs (a combination of two vowel sounds one after the other, as in the English word *house*, where the vowel starts as an 'ah' sound and finishes as an 'oo'). Many Scots words kept the older pronunciation:

Scots	Southern English
mak	make
tak	take
dee	die
craw	crow
hoose	house
coo	cow

Known by experts as the 'Great Vowel Shift', this development helped to separate the 'Inglis' of Scotland still further from the language of its southern neighbour.

Traces of the 'unshifted' way of speaking still remain in northern England today – on Tyneside, for example, you may hear *reet* and *neet* for *right* and *night*, and, famously, *toon* for *town*. But, for reasons of social class and economic advantage, the language of southern England, especially London, became the accepted way of speaking – and writing, and printing – English. In this way, quite unintentionally, it helped establish a new and separate identity for the language of the Scots.

To hear more examples of shifted vowels in English, try:
http://eweb.furman.edu/~mmenzer/gvs/

"

...en eftyr folowis ane lytil treaty of the Instruccion of the figures of armes and of the blasoning of the samyn eftir the fraynche oppinyon translatit owt of fraynche in Scottes at the Co[m]mand of an wirschepfull man Wilzim Cumyn of Inuerellochy...

British Library, MS Harley 6149, dated 1494

...hereafter follows a little treatise [handbook] of heraldic designs and the blazoning of the same [how they should be correctly displayed] after the French manner, translated out of French into Scots, at the command of a worshipful [distinguished] man, William Comyn of Inverallochy...

"

CHAPTER TWO

SCOTS – AND PROUD OF IT

'In fourteen hundred and ninety-two, Columbus sailed the ocean blue.' Many of us know that rhyme; it helps us remember an event that changed the world. But just two years later, another significant happening took place. It was maybe not quite so important, and perhaps not at all deserving to be remembered in verse, but it does mark something of a linguistic turning point. What are we talking about? The fact that, in 1494, Scottish scribe Adam Loutfut became the first known person in the universe to use the word 'Scots' to describe the language spoken by the majority of Scottish people.

This means, of course, the language formerly known as 'Inglis'; Gaelic was still the language of the Highlands and Islands.

Well done, Adam! However, our weel-respectit scribe did not intend to be revolutionary. Rather, he was famous for his neat, precise writing with quill-pen on parchment, and for his skills as a translator. But his brief remark at the beginning of an arcane text about heraldic badges and how to wear them proves that by the late 1400s, the pick-and-mix 'Inglis'-based language of the Scottish people had developed a name and an identity all of its own.

The other important thing to note about Adam is that he was a writer. He did not just speak Scots words, he wrote them down, in letters and in books. His spelling and vocabulary were not the same as ours today, but, as you can see on page 36, they were not that far apart, either.

Once a language is recorded and given a name, it increases in status – and in certainty. Written words are preserved. They can be consulted again and again, checked and compared. Writing also 'fixes' a language, at least among scribes, clerks, keepers of accounts and other literarate classes. Once readers know what words usually look like, it becomes more and more difficult to change them.

The very first texts in Scots that we know about were written down over 150 years before scribe Adam lived and worked. They include around 50 glosses (explanatory notes) written around 1340 in the margins of an older Scottish legal document, the 1312 Charter of Scone.

Local hero

And Scots were not only becoming literate, but also literary. The first major example of Scots creative writing to survive in written form is John Barbour's *The Brus*, composed in around 1370. Over 13,000 lines long (writers and their audiences had stamina in those days), *The Brus* is a poem in praise of Scots warrior king Robert the Bruce, who fought against English invaders. Barbour (1320–1395) was a churchman as well as a poet; for a while he held a post at Aberdeen Cathedral. He knew Latin and French; he had studied at Oxford and in France. But he still chose to write his greatest work in the Scots language, and to include favourite themes that would still preoccupy Robbie Burns 400 years later: patriotism, the heroic struggle of the Scottish underdog, and freedom.

A! Fredome is a noble thing.
Fredome mays man to haiff liking.
Fredome all solace to man giffis,
He levys at es that frely levys.

John Barbour, *The Brus*, c.1370, book 1

*mays man to haiff liking: gives a man choice;
solace: comfort; giffis: gives; levys: lives; es: ease.*

Meet the makars

By the time Barbour died, there was a new Scots word: *makar*. Or rather, it was an old word given a precise new meaning. A makar was an official poet, welcome at, and paid by, the Scottish royal court. Often, like Barbour, connected with the Church (the only provider of academic education in medieval Scotland), makars were viewed as skilled craftsmen, ready, able and willing to produce verses to please kings and courtiers. Scots kings from the Stewart dynasty (beginning with Robert II, 1371–1390) were keen on literature and all the arts, and liked to try their hand at it, sometimes. King James I penned a long poem telling his own true love-story, *The Kings Quhair*, around 1424 *(quhair*: book*)*. Later, his descendant James VI not only wrote several books himself – his key concerns being witchcraft and tobacco – but also, in 1584, drew up a neat set of rules for writing poetry.

Like Barbour, the makars were proud of Scotland's past, and shared a strong and sometimes prickly sense of Scottish identity. (After 1420, so could other Scots readers, thanks to Andrew of Wyntoun's *Orygynale Cronykil*, the first history book in Scots – in rhyming verse!) But the works of the makars also show that Scots thinkers and writers – however backward and barbarous their enemies believed them to be – were closely in touch with the latest European literary and cultural fashions. Strange but true: Scots royals and courtiers, wrapped in their plaids, sheltering, or scheming, behind the strong stone walls of their castles, also found time to listen to readings from works such as these:

• **1438** *The Buik of Alexander* – a romance, possibly by John Barbour, mostly adapted from an Old French text.

• **c.1456 Gilbert Hay,** *Buke of the Law of Armys* – translated from a French manual of military tactics. He also wrote a version of the *Alexander* romance.

• **c.1470 Blind Harry,** *Schir William Wallace* – a patriotic epic.

• **c.1470–1505 Robert Henryson,** *Morall Fabylls* – a retelling of Aesop's ancient Greek stories. Also *The Testament of Cresseid* – a tragic tale from ancient Greece, celebrating human courage in defiance of cruel fate and vindictive pagan gods.

• **c.1480–1515 William Dunbar,** *The Throssil* [thistle] *and the Rose* (about a royal wedding); *The Treatis of the Tua Marit Wemen and the Wedo* (in which three lower-class women discuss their husbands' shortcomings); *The Dance of the Sevin Deidlie Synnis* (as shocking as it sounds) – plus many more poems about love, romance, the royal court and low life. Dunbar's work is vivid, personal, lyrical, often touching.

• **1508 John Lydgate,** *The Complaint of the Black Knight* – a chivalric adventure. Though written by an English author, it is the earliest dated book printed in Scotland, using the latest technology, by Edinburgh pioneers Walter Chepman and Andro Myllar.

• **1531 Gavin Douglas**, *Eneados* – a translation of Virgil's *Aeneid*, an ancient Roman classic, telling the epic adventures of a warrior hero and the founding of the city of Rome.

• **1540 Sir David Lyndsay**, *Ane Pleasant Satyre of the Thrie Estaitis* – class-based social satire. The first surviving play in Scots, given its first performance in front of King James V.

The fear of death…

I that in heill was and gladness
Am trublit now with great sadness
And feblit with infirmitie:
Timor Mortis conturbat me.

Our plesance here is all vain glory,
This fals world is but transitory,
The flesh is bruckle, the Feynd is slee:
Timor Mortis conturbat me.
. . .
Unto the Death gois all Estatis:
Princis, Prelatis and Potestatis,
Baith rich and poor of all degree:
Timor Mortis conturbat me.
. . .
Sen he [Death] has all my brether tane,
He will naught let me live alane;
Of force I man his next prey be:
Timor Mortis conturbat me.

William Dunbar, *Lament for the Makars*, c.1506

*heill: health; Timor Mortis conturbat me: The fear of
Death worries me; bruckle: brittle; Feynd: Devil; slee:
sly, cunning; Estatis: classes; Prelatis: churchmen;
Potestatis: powerful people; sen: since; brether: brothers
(i.e. fellow poets); tane: taken; man: must*

Back to the future

In 2004, the Scottish Government appointed the first official Makar for centuries. The honour went to Edwin Morgan, whose works were undeniably Scottish, thankfully without being too aggressively Scots.

After Morgan died, much lamented, in 2010, the title passed to Liz Lochhead, famous not only for her irreverent wit and poems that celebrate everyday Scottish life, but also for plays that take a fresh look at Scotland's past, including *Mary Queen of Scots Got Her Head Chopped Off*.

Morgan's poems have won him enduring fame, but, since his death, his influence lives on in another way. In his will, he left almost one million pounds to the Scottish National Party, who have announced that they plan to use the money to pay for a referendum on Independence for Scotland.

Battles of words

In spite of their taste for Renaissance literature, Scots kings and nobles of the 15th and 16th centuries were still pretty warlike. Why else would they choose to enjoy poetry readings in much the same way as a boxing match? *Flytings* (bouts of verbal sparring between rival poets) were top spectator sports at the Scots royal court. As the air turned thick with insults (mostly far too racist, sexist and scatological to be quoted today), the audience applauded. The man deemed to have heaped the most shame, blame or ridicule on his opponent became top poet – for a while.

> Thow crop and rute of traitoris tressonable,
> The fathir and modir of murthour and mischief,
> Dissaitfull tyrant, with serpentis tung, unstable
> Cukcald, crawdoun, coward and common thief...

From *The Flyting of Dunbar and Kennedy*, c.1501–1513

crop and rute: seed and root; tressonable: treasonable; murthour: murder; dissaitful: deceitful; unstable: unreliable; crawdoun: cowardly, beastly (craws = *evil company*).

Scots and the Kirk

By 1500, all kinds of legal and administrative documents were being written in Scots, from marriage agreements and diplomatic letters to mortgage contracts and wage-bargains. Scots was the language of the castles, the streets, the offices and the lawcourts. It was everywhere – except the one place that mattered most.

In 1560, religious reformers in Scotland, led by the formidable John Knox, broke away from the Catholic Church in Rome to establish their own, Reformed, branch of the Christian tradition. This new body soon acquired a Scots name – the Kirk – together with a very considerable influence in politics, religious practice, and the minutest details of individual Scots' private lives. The Kirk became responsible for providing basic schooling in (almost) every Scottish village. This increased its hold on the Scottish national consciousness still further – and, unintentionally, did a great deal of damage to the Scots language.

How so? The reformers themselves were extremely well educated. And they belonged to an international community of Protestant scholars and churchmen, stretching from Norway via Switzerland to what is now the Czech Republic. At home they spoke Scots, but, to a man, when it came to important religious documents, they wrote in English.

Protestant reformers wanted people to be able to read the Bible in their own local languages. Exiled to Geneva, Switzerland, by nervous governments (north and south of the Border), a team of Protestant scholars from the British Isles pored over their dictionaries to produce a new translation. It appeared in 1560 – in English! But that was much more widely understood than the Latin of the Catholic Bible, and so the Geneva Bible was eagerly studied by Protestant ministers in Scotland. Not long afterwards, Scots King James VI (King of England as well, from 1603) commissioned a magnificent 'Authorised Version' of the Bible for his subjects to 'read, study and inwardly digest'. Published in 1611, it is a masterpiece of *English* prose.

To devout Protestant Scots, the Bible was literally the Word of God. And, even if they did not think that 'God was an Englishman', they believed that it was their pious duty to read his Word, in English, at least once a week, and often every day.

The sire turns o'er, wi patriarchal grace,
The big ha' Bible, once his father's pride;
His bonnet rev'rently is laid aside,
His lyart haffets wearing thin and bare;
Those strains that once did sweet in Zion glide,
He wales a portion with judicious care;
And 'Let us worship God!' he says with solemn air.

Robert Burns, 'The Cottar's Saturday Night', 1785

wi: with; *ha'*: sitting room (best room); *bonnet*: hat; *lyart haffets*: grey side-whiskers; *wales*: chooses; *cottar*: cottager, tenant farmer.

English was now the language of religion. The Psalms of David – the only music allowed in most Kirk services – were translated into English and set to rhythmical, memorable tunes. Scots *dominies* (schoolmasters) taught their pupils to read and write 'correct' English – and sometimes beat them if they 'lapsed' into Scots. And so, even among Scots speakers, English became special – and Scots began to be seen as second-class.

"

The noblest prospect a
Scotchman ever sees is the
high road that leads him
to London.

Dr Samuel Johnson, English writer
and lexicographer, 1709–1784

…a very corrupt Dialect of the
[English] Tongue

Scottish philosopher David Hume, 1711–1776

"

CHAPTER THREE

ON THE WAY OOT?

In 1603, King James VI of Scotland inherited the English crown and became James I of England as well. Two years later, he left Scotland and moved – or *flitted*, as the Scots say – to London. Praised by even a Scottish poet (Dunbar) as 'the flour of Cities all', London was by far the biggest, richest, busiest town in all the lands James now ruled. It was home to English monarchs, English lawcourts, and, of course, the English Parliament.

King James had been born in Scotland. He was the son of the impossibly romantic (and foolish, and tragic) Mary Queen of Scots. Like his glamorous mother and generations of royal Scottish ancestors before him, he was a fluent Scots speaker, and he had a broad Scottish accent. But his move to England was very bad news for the future of his native 'Scots tung'.

Haste ye back?

Once safely settled in London, James VI and I did not hurry back to his homeland. In fact, he hardly ever visited Scotland during the rest of his long life (he died in 1625). Looking back over the centuries, we now know that James VI was the last Scottish king to live north of the Border – and that his second son, who became Charles I, was the last king of Scotland to be able to communicate with his subjects in Scots.

Of course, ordinary people in Scotland went on speaking Scots among themselves (or Gaelic, in the Highlands and Western Islands). And very expressive it could be, too. But King James's move south marked the beginning of the end of Scots as a language of power – or even of respectability. Already, as we have seen in Chapter 2, the Kirk encouraged English. Now, following James and Charles, Scots courtiers, politicians, government officials, writers, artists and thinkers looked to London as the place where they simply had to be. And in London, everyone – even Scots – spoke English.

De'il gie ye colic, the wame o' ye, fause theif; daur ye say Mass in my lug?

Protest by Edinburgh wifie Jenny Geddes
in St Giles Cathedral, 1637

De'il: Devil; gie: give; wame: stomach; fause: false; daur: dare; lug: ear; wifie: any woman aged over about 30, not necessarily married.

Jenny was protesting about the introduction of English-style church services to Scotland, on the orders of King Charles I. But her objections were doctrinal, rather than linguistic.

Stories in song

As well as inventing splendid insults, ordinary Scots people also composed, memorised, sang and passed on a great many ballads: dramatic, tragic, gruesome, bawdy, thrilling stories in song.

The Twa Corbies

As I was walking all alane,
I heard twa corbies making a mane;
The tane unto the t'other say,
'Where sall we gang and dine to-day?'

'In behint yon auld fail dyke,
I wot there lies a new slain knight;
And naebody kens that he lies there,
But his hawk, his hound, and lady fair.

'His hound is to the hunting gane,
His hawk tae fetch the wild-fowl hame;
His lady's ta'en another mate;
So we may mak our dinner sweet.

'Ye'll sit on his white hause-bane,
And I'll pike out his bonny blue een;

Wi ae lock of his gowden hair
We'll theek our nest when it grows bare.

'Mony a one for him makes mane,
But nane sall ken where he is gane;
Oer his white banes, when they are bare,
The wind sall blaw for evermair.'

From Sir Walter Scott, *Minstrelsy of the Scottish
Border* (1802–1803)

*corbies: carrion crows; alane: alone; mane: moan (here,
it mans 'talk'); tane: one; sall: shall; yon: yonder (that
one over there); auld: old; fail dyke: turf wall (made of
slabs of turf tightly packed together); wot: know; kens:
knows, understands; hause-bane: collarbone; een: eyes;
gowden: golden; theek: thatch; makes mane: mourns.*

'The Twa Corbies' is one of the most famous
Scottish ballads. Passed on by word of mouth
from one generation to the next, many of these
songs are still known today on both sides of the
Atlantic. Narrative songs of similar character are
found in Spanish (where they are known as
romances) and in the Scandinavian languages.

'A parcel of rogues'

Just like today, powerful people with a part to play in national or international government spent a lot of their time travelling. Scots lords, landowners, lawyers and other top brass moved between Edinburgh and London. Their journey each way might last for an exhausting 10 days or more, but they felt that the effort was worth it. In London, they mostly spoke English, but once back in Scotland, they 'lapsed' into Scots for meetings of the Scottish Parliament and sessions at the Scottish lawcourts. Legal, parliamentary and many other official documents were written in Scots, as well.

But in 1707, faced by a financial crisis and tempted by the chance for a few of their number to win power and influence as MPs in London, members of the Scottish Parliament voted to suspend sittings – that is, give up their independent law-making powers. (The parliament would not meet again until 2001.) Scotland was joined to England as part of a new United Kingdom, and English, not Scots, was the national language.

Many years later, Scotland's greatest poet was still incensed by this state of affairs:

> We're bought and sold
> for English gold –
> Sic a parcel o rogues
> in a nation!

Robert Burns, 'Fareweel to A' Our Scottish Fame', 1791

sic: such.

North Britain

Scots with an eye to winning fame and fortune down south began to call themselves 'North British'. Many English people, and perhaps some Scots, too, expected them to behave just like the English, and for the Scots language to vanish or be absorbed into its bigger, 'better' neighbour. Scots began to be seen as just an incorrect version of English, not as a language in its own right. When in England, even Gaelic-speaking Highland chiefs would rather talk in 'proper' English, or even French.

The Union having incorporated two nations and rendered them one people, the distinctions which had subsisted for many ages gradually wear away, pecularities disappear; the same manners prevail in both parts of the island...the same standard of taste and purity of language is established.

William Robertson (a Scot), *History of Scotland*, 1759

To begin with, Scots speakers down south were met with bafflement, or mild hilarity, or a patronising sneer. However, after the Jacobite rebellion of 1715 in support of the Scottish Stewart (Stuart) dynasty – and especially after 1745, when Londoners feared invasion by a 'savage' Scottish army – Scots people, and Scots ways of talking, were treated with suspicion and even hostility.

The whole of the common people [of Scotland] are slaves [barbarians].

English political writer John Wilkes, 1725–1797

Helpless?

In 1763, keen young Scots nobleman's son James Boswell was introduced, in London, to Dr Samuel Johnson, compiler of the monumental *Dictionary of the English Language* (published 1755). Johnson was famous for his clumsy, untidy appearance and coarse, gruff manners, but the two men became close friends, and travelled to explore Scotland together. Hearing Boswell's Scottish accent, Johnson accused him of being a Scot.

> *Boswell:* 'I do indeed come from Scotland, but I cannot help it.'

> *Johnson:* 'That, Sir, is what a very great many of your countrymen cannot help.'

Being Scottish, having a Scots accent, or, still worse, speaking Scots, was a grave disadvantage in polite London society. Even world-class philosopher David Hume (1711–1776), who led the great flowering of rational, scientific study known as the 'Edinburgh Enlightment', felt obliged to apologise for his 'unhappy accent and pronunciation'.

Lost and found

In 1764, James Boswell – biographer, friend and travelling companion of the great Dr Samuel Johnson – lamented, 'The Scottish language is being lost every day, and in a short time will become quite unintelligible.'

Five years later, following the success of Dr Johnson's English dictionary, Boswell resolved to start work on a Scots dictionary of his own. He completed about 800 entries, but then put the project aside for a while. It was never completed.

After Boswell died, his books and papers were sold, and his unfinished dictionary disappeared. An important fragment of Scots history was lost and gone for ever – or so scholars concluded.

Imagine their delight when, in 2010, 39 pages of Boswell's missing text were rediscovered, quite by chance, in Oxford's Bodleian Library.

Out of time

Boswell would have recognised the Scots words in this list, but very few of them are still spoken today. That seems a pity. As 19th-century Scottish novelist Robert Louis Stevenson remarked (in his unfinished novel *Weir of Hermiston*), Scots can often 'tingle in the ear'.

betweesh between

boushty bed. From the Old French *boiste* 'wooden box'. Not to be confused with a **bowster** (bolster – a big feather pillow).

Fack indeed?! Oh really?! Not a sweary word – it's from *fact*.

ferntickle freckled. Freckles were thought to result from being touched by the fairies.

flumgummery foolish, frivolous

Gardyloo! Very famous; from the French *Gardez l'eau!* (Look out for the water!). Shouted when Edinburgh housewives and serving maids were about to empty chamberpots from high windows into the street below.

haggersnash scraps of meat. From **hag** 'to cut'; **snash** 'to bite'.

heididpeer of equal height

illwillie malevolent. Similarly **guidwillie** (which is also a Scots surname): generous, hearty, affable.

jimp dainty

mell mix together, mingle

mimp speak or act primly or affectedly. Probably echoes the sound made by someone speaking through primly pursed lips.

mirligoes dizziness. Perhaps related to *whirl*, **birl**, *twirl* – Scots or English, they all mean 'to spin round'.

moggan long sock or stocking

nesh bog, soft ground

pennywabble weak ale. Traditionally, the strength of Scots ale was described by referrring to the price of a whole barrel, in shillings (a silver coin, worth 12 old pennies).

Eighty-shilling ale was strong; 40-shilling ale was lighter. If you do the maths, you will see that penny ale was very weak indeed.

pilleurichie fuss and bother

pingle struggle, compete. Actually an English word, from around 400 years ago. It's disappeared from English, too – perhaps it just didn't sound convincing.

queem pleasing

ramstoorie rough and ready. From the Old French *estour* 'tumult'; *ram* adds force to the meaning.

rummelieguts windbag. The word echoes the real-life sound – or, as the experts say, it's onomatopoeic.

snowke sniff around, like a dog

> Nae doubt but they were fain o' ither,
> And unco pack and thick thegither;

fain: fond; ither: [each] other; unco: exceptionally; pack and thick thegither: close and friendly together.

Wi' social nose whyles snuff'd and snowkit;
Whyles mice an' moudiwarts they howkit;
Whyles scour'd awa' in long excursion
An' worry'd ither in diversion...

Robert Burns, 'The Twa Dogs', 1784

whyles: sometimes; snowkit: past tense of 'snowke';
moudiwarts: moles; howkit: dug up; scour'd awa': ran
off; worry'd ither in diversion: chased each other for fun.

sugg fat and lazy. A Viking word, from Orkney
Scots. Not complimentary. Viking warriors
were meant to watch their weight. If a Viking
man's belt no longer fastened around his
middle, he was in trouble.

tappietourie topmost point – anything from the
pompom on Harry Lauder's famous *bunnet*
(see page 75) to the flag flying above
Edinburgh Castle.

thigger beggar. A word from Old Norse: *þiggja*
'to receive' (the letter þ, known as 'thorn', is an
old form of *th*).

Speaking proper

In 1761 an Irish actor, Thomas Sheridan, began to hold classes in Edinburgh to teach aspiring Scottish ladies and gentlemen how to speak 'proper' English. Claiming that he found 'the dialect of the country most imperfect', he charged one guinea for each of his lectures (getting on for £100 today). They proved very popular.

Yet another *dunt* (blow) to Scots pride came when popular Scottish-born poet James Thomson left his native heath for England. His most famous work? 'Rule, Britannia'!

Readers, do not despair! Although mocked, threatened and despised, by the late 18th century the Scots language still had not completely disappeared. At home in Scotland, ordinary people outside the Highlands and Western Islands still went on speaking it; and a few determined individuals, led by genial Edinburgh wigmaker, bookseller and librarian Allan Ramsay (1686–1758) and 'Mad Lad' poet Robert Fergusson (1750–1774) made valiant efforts to preserve it.

Ramsay composed verses in Scots and English, and had great success with a play full of Scots ballads, *The Gentle Shepherd* (1725) – until the Edinburgh Kirk leaders closed the city's theatres down, claiming that they were immoral. Ramsay won even greater fame for collecting and publishing traditional Scots poems and songs. His volumes *Tea Table Miscellany* and *The Ever Green* remained popular for a hundred years and more.

Also born in *Auld Reekie* (Old Smoky – a nickname for Edinburgh that he himself invented), Fergusson studied at Dundee and then at St Andrews University, where he had many wild and disreputable adventures. Back in Edinburgh, working as a government clerk, young Fergusson spent exciting, exhausting leisure hours in the city's political and social clubs, and wrote poetry. Still high-spirited and defiant, he insisted on using broad Scots for his verses. Alas, when Fergusson was only 23 years old, he suffered a serious mental illness. Then, further tragedy, he fell downstairs, injuring his head and becoming 'insensible'. He died the next year, in Edinburgh's Bedlam (madhouse), aged only 24.

The Immortal Bard

Ramsay and Fergusson have another claim to fame: they inspired Scotland's most famous – and some still say, best – poet, Robert Burns (1759–1796). Although desperately poor, Burns's parents did their best to give their children a good education. Young Robert, a *lad of pairts* (bright boy, full of promise) if ever there was one, read widely and – inspired by a teenage sweetheart – began, aged 14, to write verse.

Burns wrote mostly in Scots, although he could, when he chose, compose in correct, elegant English, full of fashionable allusions to classical Greek and Latin culture. He was also inpired by the revolutionary movements of his day, sharing, for example, the French rebels' hope of 'Liberty, Equality and Brotherhood':

What though on hamely fare we dine,
Wear hodden grey an' a' that?

hodden grey: rough homespun cloth.

Gie fools their silks, and knaves their wine,
A man's a man for a' that.
For a' that, an' a'that,
Their tinsel show, an a' that,
The honest man, tho' e'er sae poor,
Is king of men for a' that.

'Is There for Honest Poverty', 1795

tinsel: gaudy, tawdry.

Burns was witty, charming, moody, passionate and irresponsible. He fathered at least 13 children with four or five different women. His life was full of hard work, debt and occasional deep depressions. He was patronised as a 'heaven-taught ploughman poet' by rich, fashionable men and women in Edinburgh who had infinitely less talent.

Yet Burns secured lasting fame, and a unique place at the heart of Scots culture, by his remarkable gift for expressing the deepest thoughts and feelings in a direct and simple way – and in Scots:

Altho' he has left me for greed o' the siller,
I dinna envy him the gains he can win;
I rather wad bear a' the lade o' my sorrow,
Than ever hae acted sae faithless to him.

'Altho' he has left me', 1791

siller: silver, money; dinna: do not; I rather wad: I would rather; lade: burden, weight; hae: have; sae: so.

Without whom…

Scotland also has to thank Burns for collecting and preserving many traditional Scots songs and ballads. He often used these as inspiration for his own poems, or composed new lyrics of his own to old Scots tunes. He worked closely with Edinburgh publishers George Thomson (*A Select Collection of Original Airs*, 1792) and James Johnson (*The Scots Musical Museum*, 1787–1803), although he received hardly any money for this work. But without Burns's love for the songs of his homeland, a large part of the heritage belonging to ordinary Scots-speaking people would have been lost, for ever.

Scots rebranded

By the early 19th century, some of the mistrust and fear of the Scots by the English had disappeared. Seizing his chance, ambitious Scots-speaking, Scotland-loving novelist and publisher Sir Walter Scott (1771–1832) created a whole new image for Scotland: wild, romantic, passionate, patriotic and deeply, deeply historical. In many ways, it has lasted until today.

To spread his message, Scott wrote entertaining, fast-paced novels that appealed to the huge new book-reading public of 19th-century Britain (north and south of the Border), America, the world! His plots were dramatic – shocking, even – but all in good taste and in a fine literary style. Many were based, sympathetically, on key incidents or characters in Scottish history, such as *reiver* (cattle-raider) and outlaw, Rob Roy. Any fighting against the English or plans for rebellion were safely in the past. So were topics that might excite nervousness among readers, such as calls for Scottish liberty and independence.

Scott wrote the narrative of his stories mainly in English, but several characters in his novels speak in Scots. And, however romanticised they appear, Scott's Scots are real people, with dignity and pride.

Divided selves

The same can be said of Scotland's other great 19th-century novelists, James Hogg (1770–1835) and Robert Louis Stevenson (1850–1894). Hogg's masterwork, *Confessions of a Justified Sinner*, was inspired by the Kirk's peculiarly Scottish version of the Protestant Christian tradition. Its fantastical mixture of wit, exuberance, guilt and anxiety makes 'a window into Scotsmen's souls' like few other works.

Stevenson's novels cover a wide range of topics, from Scottish history (the 1745 Jacobite rebellion in *Kidnapped*) to the sinister disintegration of a man's personality when confronted by uncritical fame, unbridled vice, and substance abuse, in the forward-looking *Dr Jekyll and Mr Hyde*.

Oot in the kailyard

Just as popular as Scott's and Stevenson's classic novels – although panned by most critics at the time – were collections of stories about everyday Scots life penned by a group of writers collectively known as the 'Kailyard School' (*kailyard*: kitchen garden, vegetable plot). Its most famous members included two Scots clergymen – John Watson (1850–1907), whose pen name was Ian MacLaren, and R. S. Crockatt (1859–1914) – and also J. M. Barrie (1860–1937), who wrote as 'Gavin Ogilvie', and who later became world-famous as the author of *Peter Pan*.

Kailyard stories and short novels made much greater use of the Scots language than Scott's and Stevenson's more literary works. Their chief subject matter was ordinary life in Lowland Scotland. (The most famous was, perhaps, Barrie's *A Window in Thrums*, set in small-town Kirriemuir.) They were unashamedly nostalgic, looking back to tranquil, contented country communities that had perhaps never existed – at a time when rural Scotland was being transformed by canals, railways, city growth and massive industrialisation. (These changes were hardly ever mentioned in Kailyard texts.)

In tone, the stories were moral and deeply sentimental – just like many 19th-century paintings of Scottish country scenes. They praised 'traditional' Scottish virtues approved by the writers: hard work, respect for education, thrift, religious duty. Critics called them quaint, trivial and unrealistic, but they were very popular, especially among Scots from country families now living in big cities, and among communities of emigrants who had left Scotland to live overseas. Perhaps they presented a picture of Scots life – in the Scots language – that many Scottish people liked to think was true.

Tartan tomfoolery

Singer and comic actor Sir Harry Lauder (1870–1950) was one of the most popular music-hall entertainers of the early 20th century, throughout Britain and beyond. Born to a poor family, he worked as a coalminer and in a flax factory before making a career on the stage. He had a good, clear voice, but it was his sentimental songs with catchy tunes, together with his cheerful, indomitable stage personality, that won him so many admirers. He was the first UK artiste to sell a million records, and was knighted by King George V for his work entertaining the troops during World War I (1914–1918).

For many Scottish people, Lauder's songs provided a soundtrack to everyday life. His lyrics, in a blend of English and Scots, celebrated straightforward joys:

> I love a lassie,
> A bonnie Hielan' lassie…

and gave vent to bitter heartache, combined with dour Scots determination:

> Keep right on to the end of the road,
> Keep right on to the end…

as Lauder wrote after his only son was tragically killed in battle.

However, Lauder's *pawky* (merry, roguish, shrewd) stage personality was not universally admired. Some Scots strongly disliked the 'tartan tomfoolery' that was Lauder's stage costume. (He wore a kilt, sporran, hairy woollen stockings, an outsize *bunnet* (flat cap, rather like a beret) and carried an excessively rustic twisted walking stick.) They thought that Lauder's act and many of his songs – about the hills, the heather, and simple Scotsmen and women – trivialised Scots culture and created demeaning sterotypes of Scottish people and the Scots language they spoke every day.

Revival!

In the early 20th century, a group of Scottish writers set out to 'reclaim' Scots from the sentimental backwater of the Kailyard school and the 'bonnie Scotland' image of Harry Lauder. They despised the nostalgic heritage industry that had grown up around the 'immortal memory' of Robert Burns. They were influenced by 'modernist' literary trends – realism, plain speaking and experiments with style – from continental Europe.

Famous members of this 'Scottish Literary Revival' included Lewis Grassic Gibbon, Edwin Muir, Neil Gunn and Fionn MacColla. Their informal leader, Christopher M. Grieve (1892–1978), who wrote as Hugh MacDiarmid, was a founding member of the Scottish National Party (1928), and was determined to fight against the patronising attitude of England towards Scotland, and the overpowering influence of English on the Scots language. He wrote in *Lallans* (Lowlands), a deliberately literary, not to say highbrow, version of Scots, that looked back to the vigorous, flyting language of the long-dead makars at the Scottish royal court. MacDiarmid's most famous poem, *A Drunk Man Looks at the Thistle*, is a long meditation about the nature of 'Scottishness', and a rather despairing call to Scots to reclaim their lives, their souls – and their words.

Though Scots Revival writers appealed only to a literary minority, their influence can still be felt today in the works of more popular authors who write in Scots, including Irvine Welsh of *Trainspotting* fame.

A calmer, less political approach to the study and preservation of Scots language and culture came with the setting up in 1951 of the School of Scottish Studies at Edinburgh University. Inspired by the work of pioneering US folklorist Alan Lomax, its teams of students and scholars were just in time to collect and record a vast archive of Scots anecdotes, reminiscences and reflections on everyday life in the first half of the 20th century, together with songs, songs, songs.

And so, 'dying' Scots was saved again. But what of the language today, and in the future?

'We're all Jock Tamson's bairns.'

(proverb)

The brotherhood of man (and woman), with a particularly Scottish flavour.

A' THE GO

A' the go: popular.

In spite of its troubled history, Scots survives! Almost everywhere in Scotland, you can still hear Scots words being spoken. And you can read them on the Internet, or listen to them on radio and TV. Even in Gaelic-speaking districts of the Highlands and Western Islands, the English spoken to outsiders is peppered with Scots vocabulary. Scots text can be quoted in the Scottish Parliament, although 'as a matter of courtesy' advance notice must be given by MSPs intending to make long speeches in Scots, so that arrangements can be made for their words to be translated.

Mony weys

In 2009, a guide to some of the workings of the Scottish Parliament was translated into Scots and appeared on the Parliament's website:

> Ye hae mony weys tae mak yir views kent whan ye hae strang feelins aboot issues. This leaflet will help ye finn oot mair aboot the Pairlament and weys tae involve yirsel in its wark…

The leaflet was part of an initiative with the best of democratic intentions that also provided public information in Arabic, Bengali, Chinese, French, German, Italian, Polish, Punjabi, Russian, Spanish and Urdu. But it was roundly mocked by English newspapers and criticised by some Scottish language experts. As of 2017, it seems to have disappeared…

A little book like this can only hope to give a brief taste of the Scots that is widely spoken today. And it's perhaps not by chance that many of the most common Scots words and phrases are about ordinary, everyday life: friends and family, homes, clothes, the weather, and, above all, food. When speaking about what really matters, Scots stick with Scots. They also find Scots very useful when expressing their feelings, especially if they feel *crabbit* (grumpy), *fushionless* (dull), or *up to high doh* (over-excited).

On the following pages we'll take a *keek* (peer, look) at some of those everyday words.

Family and friends

auntie aunt; **aye ma auntie**: I don't believe you.

bairn child. *Brunt [burnt] bairns dreid aye [always] the fire* (proverb).

bidie-in: live-in lover. Not to be confused with *wifie* (see page 53) or indeed with *wife*.

billie brother

callart youngster

chiel young person

> Facts are chiels that winna ding [fight].
>
> Robert Burns, 'A Dream', 1786

(You can't fight facts.)

dochter daughter

faither father. *A kent his faither*: Crushing Scots put-down: 'I knew his father' = 'He's a junior/inferior to me.'

jo sweetheart. Famously used in one of Robert Burns's most touching love poems. Here is the final verse:

John Anderson, my jo, John,
We clamb the hill thegither
And monie a cantie day, John,
We've had wi' ane anither:
Now we maun totter down, John,
And hand in hand we'll go,
And sleep together at the foot,
John Anderson my jo.

clamb: climbed; thegither: together; cantie: happy; ane anither: one another; maun: must.

loon young man; **orra loon:** odd-job boy; spare pair of hands.

mither mother

wean (= **wee ane**) child. As in 'Maw, Paw and the Weans', the archetypal Broon family, created in Dundee in 1936, and still going strong in comic strips in the popular *Sunday Post* newspaper. *Maw Broon's Cookbook* was a surprise recent Christmas bestseller.

wenching courting. Very medieval-sounding, but still used today:

Neighbour, on bus: 'Do you know what X has been getting up to?'
Other neighbour, cautiously: 'Well, I'd heard that she has a new friend…'
First neighbour, with emphasis: 'Aye, *wenching*.'

Nice words

bonnie beautiful. Can be used of males as well as females.

My bonnie lies over the ocean,
My bonnie lies over the sea,
My bonnie lies over the ocean,
O bring back my bonnie to me.

Traditional Scottish song, origins unknown; 'bonnie' may perhaps refer to Bonnie Prince Charlie, leader of the 1945 Jacobite rebellion.

braw fine, brave. *He's a braw fechter [fighter]!*

canny cautious, sensible; **ca' canny**: be careful.

cantie cheerful, happy

couthie friendly, pleasant

> Where are the folk like the folk of the West –
> Cantie and couthie and kindly, the best?

> From the song 'Westering Home', composed by
> Hugh Roberton (1874–1952), founder of the
> once very famous Glasgow Orpheus Choir

Gaun, yersel! Well done! Go on!

grippie thrifty. *A grippie hand will never want*
(proverb).

kenspeckle well-known; like *weel-kent*, implies
respect.

lang-heidit wise

pawky drily humorous, crafty, roguish

sonsie comfortable, plump.

> Fair fa' your honest, sonsie face,
> Great chieftain of the puddin-race!

> Robert Burns, 'Address to a Haggis', 1786

> *fair fa': good luck to*

weel-kent well-known

Nasty words

birkie person full of his own importance

> Ye see yon birkie ca'd a lord,
> Wha struts an' stares, an' a' that,
> Thou' hundreds worship at his word,
> He's but a coof [fool] for a' that.

Robert Burns, 'Is There, for Honest Poverty', 1795

deil the devil. *The deil tak the hindmost! The deil's aye guid til his own!* (proverbs)

dour stern, sullen, grim. Can describe people, the weather, the state of the nation…

feartie coward

gawkit clumsy

girn moan or whinge. Often used to describe fretful children.

glaikit foolish, thoughtless

gomeril ignorant, thoughtless person. *Ye big gomeril!* Another word with a similar meaning is **neuchtie**.

greeting crying. *She was greetin' like a bairn who'd lost a' his sweeties.* Perhaps Norse, perhaps Old English. A **greeting face** is permanently miserable; a tired, tense or over-emotional encounter can end in a **greeting match**.

hallirackit rowdy

heckle jeer at, attack verbally. This Scots word, which originally meant to break or strip flax stalks for use in the linen-weaving industry, is now familiar to politicians and stand-up comedians wordwide.

jessie (usually **big jessie**) feeble, cowardly man. Often said fairly kindly: *Don't be a big jessie. Jessie* is a familiar form of the popular Scottish female name Janet.

minky/manky disgusting

row a telling-off. *Do that homework or ye'll get a row from the teacher.*

scunnered absolutely disgusted. *I'm fair scunnered wi those yins [that lot].*

shoogly shaky, unsteady. But Shooglenifty is

the very descriptive name of a Scottish folk-rock band.

skelp hit. *I'll gie ye a skelpit lug [ear]!*

sleekit sleek, but also devious. The English *smooth* has rather the same resonance, but *sleekit* is somehow much more meaningful.

stammygaster nasty shock

teuchter Highlander; slow, stupid country-dweller. Offensive – almost the Scots equivalent of the N-word in the USA.

unco extremely; **unco guid**: holier than thou.

> O ye wha are sae guid yoursel,
> Sae pious and sae holy,
> Ye've nought to do but mark and tell
> Your neebours' fauts and folly!

Robert Burns, 'Address to the Unco Guid', 1786

wabbit feeble, exhausted

And remember:

Whit's fur ye'll no go by ye! You'll get what's coming to you!

Insults

The Scots are good at these. Here are just a few:

Awa' an bile yer heid. Naff off!

Dinnae fash yersel/Dinnae dee yer bunnet!
Temper, temper!

gaein all tae staps falling to pieces
(metaphorically as well as literally).

Haud yer wheesht! Shut up!

**He could start a rammie [quarrel] in an empty
room**. He's extremely quarrelsome.

I could see him far enough. I am extremely
annoyed with him.

Let him dree his weird. Let him suffer the
consequences of his own actions; the Scots
version of karma, perhaps? But also, more
stoically, *We maun thole our weird*: We must
endure what fate sends us.

Meg wi' the muckle mou woman who talks too
much. Recently revived as an uncomplimentary
nickname for a Scots MSP.

She kens the right side of a bawbee [halfpenny]!
She's mean.

Who stole your scone? What a misery!

Yer heid is full of broken bottles! Your over-
ambitious plans will not work.

**Ye've an eye in yer heid like a stinkin' haddie
[haddock]!** You've done that job all crooked.

And, as a not-so-tactful hint to an unwelcome guest:

Here's yer hat,
what's yer hurry?

Food and drink

'Hunger or burst' is about more than food. A feature of the Scots outlook on life, perhaps?

bannock flat roll or (dry, unsweetened) cake, traditionally made with barley. *A bannock's better than nae breid.*

blaeberry bilberry, blueberry

> I left my baby lying there,
>   lying there, lying there,
> I left my baby lying there
> And went to gather blaeberries.

> Scottish folksong which describes how a baby was snatched away by the fairies, never to be seen again. Known to have reduced many a sensitive child to tears.

bramble blackberry

breid bread. *Her breid's baken*: She's got it made.

buttery (buttery rowie) a flaky roll, originally baked with butter. The Scots equivalent of a croissant.

SCOTTISH WORDS

caller fresh and wholesome

> Wha'll buy my caller herrin'?
> They're bonnie fish and halesome fairin'.
> Buy my caller herrin',
> Fresh-caught frae the Forth.'

Song by Scottish poet Carolina Oliphant (Lady
Nairne, 1766–1845) based on street-cries by
fisher-women; music by legendary Scottish
fiddler, Niel Gow (1727–1807)

fairin': food, eating.

carry-oot takeaway meal

champit mashed; **champit neeps** or **bashed
neeps** is the traditional accompaniment to
haggis.

clapshot bashed neeps combined with champit
tatties, onions, and butter or dripping. A recipe
from Orkney.

clootie dumpling a pudding made with flour,
dried fruit and spices, wrapped in a floured
cloot (cloth) and then boiled. Warming and
sustaining, but hardly light on the stomach.

crappit heids cods' heads stuffed with scraps of fish, breadcrumbs or oatmeal, onions and pepper. Economical, but thankfully no longer an everyday dish.

creesh fat (noun)

dochandoris (Gaelic: *deoch-an-doruis* 'drink at the door') a drink 'for the road' (most ill-advised, and very likely illegal); also the name of the cup that it is drunk from.

dram a drink, especially of whisky. Originally a *drachm* was a very small measure, used by apothecaries, but today in Scotland a *wee dram* can mean anything from a thimbleful to a brimming tumbler. The same applies to:

drappie or **wee drappie** a drop

farl a roughly trianglar piece of scone, bannock or oatcake; the shape is created when circular baked goods are divided into quarters, sixths or eighths.

finnan haddie gutted, salted, hot-smoked haddock. A delicacy.

fish supper fish and chips, eaten at any time of
the day or night. And the fish will be haddock
or whiting, not cod or plaice.

Supper means all kinds of food eaten with chips,
for example a pie supper, a pizza supper, a
haggis supper, a kebab supper… At their local
takeaways, Scots can also purchase dieticians'
nightmares such as chips with grated cheese.

An early-evening meal, without chips but very
often including fish, grilled, poached or fried, is
traditionally known as a **high tea** or (in
Glasgow) a **knife-and-fork tea**. Bread and
butter, scones and cakes are served as well.

fou drunk; **fou as a puggie**: drunk as a monkey;
extremely drunk

ginger any fizzy drink, whatever flavour – even
the astonishing Irn-Bru

haggis sheep's heart, lungs, etc., minced very
fine, mixed with oatmeal, onions, herbs and
spices, stuffed into a sheep's stomach and
boiled. In spite of its humble ingredients, in the
past this was a luxury dish for poor Scots who
could not afford to eat meat. From the French

verb *hâcher* 'to chop'. Today, an international symbol of Scotland.

hough shin of beef; stewed, or used to make Scotch broth. You have to be Scots, or good at learning accents, to be able to say this properly.

ingin onion. *An ingin ane an a':* [Please may I have] an onion one as well? (Say: *An inn-jinn ain an aw*.) Reputed to be said when asking for a **bridie** – a speciality of the town of Forfar. Bridies are circles of pastry filled with minced meat, and, sometimes, chopped onions. They are folded to make a half-moon shape, then baked in the oven.

jeely jam; **jeely piece**: bread and jam, or jam sandwich. A very weel-respectit minister and his wife set up the famous Jeely Piece Club to provide care – and fun, and nourishing food – for children in a deprived area of Glasgow.

kail various plants of the cabbage family; among the few vegetables positively to thrive in the Scottish climate. *Dinna scaud your mou wi' other folk's kail.*

neeps swedes – big, orange, often fed to cattle

SCOTTISH WORDS

pancake flour, eggs, milk, sugar beaten together
to make a thick battter and dropped in small
spoonfuls onto a hot **girdle** (griddle). Cooked
in a minute or two and typically served with
butter and jeely (jam). Golden syrup is
sometimes added; mysteriously, it gives the
outside a velvety texture. South of the Border,
sometimes called a *drop scone*.

pan drop a hard sugar sweet, like a large mint
imperial. The author's father, when a wee boy,
nearly choked to death on one of these. His life
was saved by an old lady in the village who had
the presence of mind to pick him up by his feet
and shake him.

pan-loaf a person with inflated ideas of their
own importance. Pan loaves (individually
shaped and baked) were superior to **plain
breid**: batch loaves which were baked very
close together and had crust only on the top
and the bottom.

parritch porridge. In literature (although not, in
the author's experience, in real life), sometimes
spoken of in the plural.

The halesome Parritch, chief o' Scotia's food…

> Robert Burns, 'The Cottar's
> Saturday Night', 1786

They're fine, halesome food – they're grand
food, parritch.

> Robert Louis Stevenson, *Kidnapped*, 1886

Save yer breath tae cool yer parritch!: Oh, do be
quiet!

partan crab; **partan-faced**: ugly

piece slice of bread, or sandwich. Also a snack.

poke paper bag. **The shakins o the poke**: the
last child in a family.

purvey refreshments served after a funeral – a
matter of honour, as well as hospitality.

saut salt

scone (say: 'scon', not 'scohn') Perhaps the best-
known example of Scots baking. Flour, butter,
baking powder, sour milk perhaps, and maybe
dried fruit. Every cook has his or her own
secret recipe. A light hand is essential.

skirlie (skirl in the pan) oatmeal and onions
fried together in an open pan. Like many
traditional Scots dishes, made with humble
ingredients but needing a skilled cook to
produce something palatable.

sourocks leaves from the sorrel plant,
traditionally nibbled when thirsty. They have a
sharp, lemony, *wersh* flavour.

stovies potatoes cooked very slowly with scraps
of meat and/or dripping. A frugal dish,
traditionally made on Mondays with the
leftovers (if any) of Sunday's dinner. Onions
optional.

syboes spring onions

tablet, taiblet an incredibly sweet confection,
like hard, gritty fudge, made by boiling
condensed milk and sugar together.

tatties potatoes; **mince and tatties**: stewed
minced beef with boiled potatoes – a never-fail
dish with almost all Scotsmen over a certain
age; **tattie bogle**: scarecrow; **tattie-howkin**: a
week's holiay in autumn, traditionally given to

children and workers so that potatoes could be
dug up for winter food.

tumshies turnips (i.e. swedes)

well-fired (of bread or rolls) over-cooked, with
a blackened surface. A Glasgow speciality;
incomprehensible (and inedible) to many
other Scots.

wersh either insipid, or tart

Ye'll have had your tea. What Scots from
everywhere else accuse Edinburgh people of
saying in order to avoid sharing food and drink
with visitors.

*And if these Scots words have maybe made you feel
hungry, you might say:*

A doot ma stammick thinks ma thrapple's been cut awthegither!

*I fear my stomach thinks my throat's been
cut altogether!*

Clothes and appearance

Yir face and parsley!: Oh yeah? (Implies that someone has made an effort to look attractive.)

bahookie bottom; a synonym is **hurdies**. More crudely, **Yer erse is oot the windae** (You don't know what you are talking about).

breeks trousers, or underpants. In spite of the popular image, most Scotsmen have worn breeks (not kilts) for centuries.

brogues shoes decorated with a pattern of punched drainage holes, pinked (zigzag) edges and sometimes tassels. Based on ancient Highland shoes, which were wrapped around the foot and tied.

bunnet hat (see page 75).

claes clothes. *Back to auld claes and porridge*: back to humdrum life after a holiday or exciting event.

corrie-fisted left-handed

fauchie pale and sickly

fur coat and nae knickers proud but fallen on hard times, *or* pretentious, *or* 'no better than she should be'.

hap up wrap up warmly. *Hap yoursel up in this plaid, the wind's gey snell [very bitter].*

meikle, muckle big. *Yon Edinburgh Parliament building's a muckle great stramash [disaster]!*

neb nose. *Keep yer neb oot my business!*

oxter armpit. *He's up to his oxters in trouble.*

pap breast. The name of many Scottish mountains, notably the Paps of Jura.

peely-wallie pale; weak and feeble. The feeling is just like this sounds.

pinkie little finger. A word originally from the Netherlands.

plaid a warm woollen wrap; *not* a tartan pattern.

plooks pimples

sannies gym-shoes

sark shirt, undershirt or petticoat. Cutty Sark

(short shirt) is the name of the sonsie young witch who dances semi-naked in a churchyard in Burns's 'Tam O' Shanter' (c.1790).

semmit vest

shoon shoes; English poets have found it a handy rhyme-word:

> Slowly, silently, now the Moon
> Walks the night in her silver shoon.
>
> Walter De La Mare (1873–1958), 'Silver'

skelf a spinter of wood sunk into the skin and causing inflammation

skippet, skeppit peaked: *a skeppit cap.*

skrankie scrawny

stoater a very good-looking girl. *See her! What a wee stoater!*

tackety studded with nails. **Tackety-boots** were hobnailed boots worn by generations of Scots schoolboys, working men and army squaddies.

tam, tammie a large floppy beret, relatively recently (1790) nicknamed 'Tam O' Shanter'

after the hero of Robert Burns's poem. Now
part of army uniform for some Scottish
battalions: Highlanders wear the fabric in their
tams sloping backwards, Lowlanders tilt it to
the right. The pompom on top is a **toorie**.

A good time

blether chatter. *We had a rare blether.* But *You're
blethering*: You're talking nonsense.

box accordion. One of the most popular Scots
instruments: loud, expressive, portable and – in
the right hands – excellent for dancing to.

ceilidh (pronounced 'KAY-lee') a party with
music and, sometimes, dancing. Originally a
Gaelic word, now also used by Scots speakers.

cleik an' gird old-fashioned hoop and stick – a
children's game

crack, craik conversation, chatter, usually
cheerful and witty. Also refers to the general
ambiance of a gathering. *Och! The craik was good
at wee Flora's the night.*

fiddle never 'violin'.

fitba (the ane wi the round ba) *the* Scottish
sport. Sometimes – in Glasgow – unpleasantly
mixed up with sectarian politics. The city's two
main teams, Rangers and Celtic (pronounced
'SEL-tick'), are based in working-class districts
traditionally 'belonging' to rival communities of
Protestants and Roman Catholics. Not to be
confused with:

footer potter idly without achieving much

golf, gowf we all know this one. But there's also
putt (originally meaning 'nudge') and **stymied**
(obstructed; originally **stime** 'unable to see').

heedrum-hodrum dismissive description of the
sort of anodyne Scots music played on TV on
New Year's Eve. The word imitates the sound.

hoachin very, very crowded. *The howf [see below]
was hoachin!*

howf friendly meeting-place, especially a pub

jauries the game of marbles

jink twisting and turning; a quick change of
direction

jouk duck out of the way

keepie-uppie kicking or heading a fitba/futba to keep it in the air. However, *The ba's on the slates*: You're in real trouble.

loup jump or leap. *Jink, joup* and *loup* can all be used to describe athletes, footballers or dancers.

mollach mess around

mouthie harmonica

peever hopscotch

pipes, the (always 'the pipes') bagpipes. And, referring to bagpipes or any other kind of pipe: *That'll put his gas at a peep*: That'll show him!

shinty the other Scottish winter sport, especially in the Highlands. A fast and furious game, rather like hockey.

stravaigin wandering

Things not going well? Then you might say:

The game's a bogie: It's a dead loss; also **It's a sair fecht.**

The weather

airts compass directions

> Of a' the airts the winds can blaw
> I dearly like the west,
> For there the bonnie lassie lives,
> The lassie I love best.
>
> Robert Burns, 'Of A' The Airts', 1790

blaw: blow

back end autumn; also **hairst** (harvest).

black as the Earl of Hell's weskit awfully dark

dreich dull, grey, damp, chill, utterly miserable
– Scots weather at its worst

drookit extremely wet; wet through. *Jings
Crivvens! [euphemism for 'Jesus Christ'] Ah'm fair
drookit!*

flaggie snowflake

fret cold, wet mist rolling in from the sea

gloaming dusk; can be a magical time in the
Scots countryside.

gurlie stormy, dangerous

> 'I saw the new moon late yestreen
> With the old moon in her arm;
> And if we go to sea, master,
> I fear we'll come to harm.'
>
> They had not sailed a league, a league,
> A league but barely three,
> When the lift grew dark, and the wind
>   blew loud,
> And gurly grew the sea.
>
> The ankers brake and the top-masts lap,
> It was such a deadly storm;
> And the waves came o'er the broken ship
> Till all her sides were torn.

> From the ballad 'Sir Patrick Spens',
> first printed in 1765

lift: sky; lap: sprang apart.

haar mist from the east (i.e. the North Sea)

mochie warm, moist, clammy

Northern Lights the aurora borealis, often
visible in Scotland in winter. True story:

Villager, to neighbour: 'See yon light in the sky?'
Educated neighbour, wishing to impress: 'Ah! The
  aurora borealis!'
Deaf old lady, arriving: 'Wha did ye jist say
  aboot that auld bugger Wallace?'

Wallace was the name of the local big farmer.

pishing raining heavily

plowetery wet and muddy

plump a shower

scudder a sudden blast of cold rain and/or wind

shaela hoarfrost; a word from Orkney. Also, the
'frosted' colour of some Shetland sheep's wool.

simmer dim the extended twilight around
midsummer in northern latitudes, when it
barely gets dark. The author has sat by a
window at about 57°N at midnight and found
enough light to read by.

smirr drizzle

snell bitterly cold

soft, sawft gentle, pleasant (even if raining);

cynically: 'really quite nice compared with what it's usually like'.

sterrn, starrn stars

stoating raining so heavily that the drops bounce off the ground

watergaw patch of rainbow in the sky

Hoose and hame

biggin building

but and ben humble two-roomed cottage (**but**: outer room, kitchen; **ben**: inner room, sitting room). Similarly **ben the hoose**: indoors.

chap knock at the door

close entrance to a tenement; also back street; row of houses; block of tenements

cludgie lavatory

cowp rubbish heap; also **coup out** 'throw away'

cundy drain

drying green communal lawn at the back of a

tenement block or group of houses, where
housewives used to hang their washing to dry

dunnie cellar or dark passageway

fantoosh over-elaborate. *Her new curtains look
awfu fantoosh.*

flit move house

four-in-a-block fairly large building containing
four self-contained flats, two upstairs, two
down. Found in Scottish cities.

hame home; **hamely**: cosy or unpretentious;
gaun hame: dying

hoose, house anything from a cottage to a
mansion (neither of which is much used in Scots)

lobby dosser homeless person who sleeps in the
entrance lobby of a tenement. Also the name of
a popular cartoon character.

lum chimney. *Lang may your lum reek [smoke]*:
May you have lasting prosperity.

midden rubbish heap

mingerator midden-raker

oose fluff, usually under the bed

roup auction of farmyard or household goods, often after a bankruptcy or other misadventure

scaffie dustman, refuse collector

skoosh squirt or slosh water, as when washing a kitchen floor

sneck latch of a gate; also **snib**

stay live, dwell permanently: *Whaur does he stay?*

steamie communal wash-house/laundry, once found in big Scottish cities. Not used today, except in the phrase *the talk of the steamie*: the latest gossip or scandal.

stob wooden fence-post

stoor dust; **stoor-sooker**: vacuum cleaner

tenement tall apartment block. Once a very common form of housing in Scottish towns and cities. Whole families lived in a *room wi a kitchen* (which was a sort of cupboard on the stair landing, with a sink and a cold tap). The shared lavatory was usually on a landing.

vennel alleyway

wallie made of clay; hence **wallie close**:
  entrance lobby to a tenement, lined with
  decorative glazed earthenware tiles (a sign of
  refinement); **wallie dugs**: china ornaments,
  usually a pair of spaniels, designed to sit on a
  mantelshelf (also a sign of refinement; now, to
  some, retro-chic; to others, ridiculous).

wynd narrow street

Wee beasties
and other wildlife

bonxie great skua (a seabird). Famous for
  defending itself against predators by spitting
  regurgitated food at them.

bubbly-jock male turkey. *Ah'm sair hauden doun
  by the bubbly-jock*: I am oppressed by many
  worries.

cattiewurrie fight. Scots cats sometimes go **ron-
  ron** (like French felines) or even **birl-birl**. If
  they do purr, they say *puhhrrrrrrrr*, not *per*.

chookie chicken

cleg horsefly; its bite is very nasty, like a **jag** (injection) or **jaggies** (stinging nettles).

collieshangie noisy argument. The general Scots word for a collie, or any other canine, is **dug**. The author knows of a collie rather wittily named 'Doug'.

corbie carrion crow; see the ballad on pages 54–55. Also called **craw**: *Ding doun the nests and the craws will flie awa.*

doo, or **cushie doo** dove, wood pigeon. Not to be confused with **coorie doon** which means 'snuggle down' – said, or sung, to restless children to encourage them to go to sleep.

emmet ant; also **pismire**.

forkie or **forkietail** earwig. Also known by very many other local names.

gimmer female sheep between one and two years old. Other ovine terms include **yowe**: ewe; **hog** or **hogget**: male one-year-old sheep; **tup**: ram; **sheepshank**: sheep's leg; **sheep**

money: farmworker's wages; **sheep's purls**: sheep dung. **Fank** is an enclosure into which sheep are herded; hence **fankled** 'trapped, entangled'.

gowan daisy. *Not care a gowan*: not care even a little bit.

gowk cuckoo. **Gowk Day**: 1 April. To **hunt the gowk**, or **be a huntegowk**: to be the butt of an April Fool joke or prank, or to be sent on a fool's errand. **Gowk storm**: springtime storm, fuss over nothing (equivalent to English 'storm in a teacup').

hoodie hooded crow. A black crow with grey markings on the head and shoulders. Rarely found south of Edinburgh – or Moscow.

hoolet owl, especially barn owl

hurcheon hedgehog

ked tick; nasty boodsucking creature, related to the spider family.

kye cattle; plural of **coo**. *A guid coo can hae an ill cauf*: Don't count your chickens.

laverock skylark

midge tiny biting insect that can cause intense skin irritation; Scotland's secret weapon.

puddock frog; **heid puddock**: the boss (also **high heid yin** [one]); cf. **mannie**: person in an official position (*the mannie from the council*).

selkie seal. Grey seals and common seals are found all round the coast of Scotland. Also the name of a magical creature in many Scottish myths and legends: a seal that transforms itself into a beautiful woman (or handsome man), loves or marries a human, and then slips away, leaving the lover heartbroken. These selkies are musical, with lovely voices.

slater, sclater woodlouse

spuggie sparrow. But NB also the traditional nonsense rhyme:

> There were twa spugs, sitting on a barra;
> One was a sprogue, the other a sparra.

tod fox

Izzatamarraonyerbarraclarra?

Question famously asked by Glasgow comedian
Stanley Baxter (see page 123)

Is that a marrow on your barrow, Clara?

Chapter Five

LOCAL VARIATIONS

As the old song declares: 'It's not what you say but the way that you say it'. That's certainly true of Scots. Although Scotland is not a large country, and Scots is not spoken in every single *neuk* (corner), there has still been room for several very different varieties of the language to develop.

Naturally, each local version of Scots has been strongly influenced by the character and history of its home region. And the dialects can be surprisingly different. What's called a *cappie* in Aberdeen, for example, is known as *pokey hat* in Glasgow (that's an ice-cream cornet). This chapter will look at some of the different dialects of Scots: the nearly-Norse language of Orkney and Shetland, the Irish-immigrant-influenced Glasgow patter, and more. Not forgetting Ullans, the Scots spoken in Northern Ireland, of course.

Weegie words

Perhaps the most famous – or infamous – Scots dialect is spoken in Scotland's biggest city, Glasgow. Fallen on hard times (though now busily recreating itself), Glasgow is proud of its great industrial past, and of its outgoing, outspoken citizens.

Glaswegian Scots – also known as *Glesga* or *Glesgha patter* (never pronounced 'GLAHZ-goe'!) – is fast, frank and (sometimes) furious. Although obscenities can abound in the mouths of neds, sengas and buckies (see below) – plus fitba fans, of course – they are often included to give emphasis, rather than to offend. And, thanks to the energetic Glasgow way of speaking, even the most friendly *Weegie* sentences can sometimes seem threatening, and/or impossible for outsiders to follow.

The difficulty comes because Glaswegians raise and lower the pitch of their voices quite dramatically as they speak. And they tend to string and slur words together in one long tangle, *byrreway* (by the way). Glesga syntax (sentence structure) also includes a sometimes baffling use of negatives, such as *Gonna nae do that* (Please don't do that!) or *Ah'm no doin naethin neither* (I'm not doing anything), together with contradictions such as: *Come oan, get awff!* Dazed and confused? Then copy one of Glasgow's many imaginative idioms (another problem for outsiders), and say *Ma heid's mince!*

Perhaps surprisingly, Glesga patter contains fewer purely Scots words than many other Scottish dialects. This is because it was shaped, in the 19th century, by English-speaking immigrants from Ireland who came to work in Glasgow industries. But even so, Glesga-speakers still have many wonderful words and phrases of their own. Here are just a few – although, be warned: not all are suitable for polite company.

Glasgow words

auldyin old person (**yin**: one).

besom (pronoucned 'BIZZ-um') a spirited or forceful woman. Can imply approval or abuse.

bowfin extremely smelly (or throbbing)

Buckie the infamous Buckfast Tonic Wine, or an alcoholic person (a.k.a. an **alkie**).

chib a knife or other weapon carried by neds

chin enquire

clap pat. *Gie the nice duggie a wee clap, hen!*

clarty dirty

close an entrance lobby to a tenement; an alley.

Doon-the-Watter Down the Water (i.e. river). Traditionally, where Glaswegians went on their holidays: a boat trip to seaside resorts close to the mouth of the River Clyde.

gallus bold, confident, dashing, cheeky, sharp. Scottish broadcaster Muriel Gray once ran a TV company called Gallus Besom.

geggie mouth

Glesga ferr (fair) the traditional start of the
  Glasgow factory holiday fortnight, in late July

Glesga kiss headbutt

jiggered exhausted

keelie tough Glasgow working man

keep the heid don't panic!

laldy *gie it laldy*: make a big effort

malky razor or sharp knife

ned lout or petty criminal. Often claimed to be
  an acronym (Non-Educated Deliquent), the
  nickname is at least 100 years old.

nippy sweetie sharp-tongued or bad-tempered
  woman

numpty fool

nyaff (usually **wee nyaff**) nasty piece of work;
  the female equivalent is a **wee herry** (hairy).

rammie argument

Scottish Words

randan drinking spree

schemie person from a deprived area (especially from a **scheme** – an area of council housing)

See you! Now look here!

senga a female ned (backslang from Agnes)

single-end small, one-roomed apartment in a tenement

sit-ooterie conservatory or sun-room

snachter something nice to eat; a treat

square go a fight in which both sides are equal

Stoap bumpin your gums! Be quiet!

stooshie uproar, controversy

ya bas you bastard(s)! *Ye're deid, ya bas!*: I really am most displeased with you.

But – very important – Glaswegians don't share many other typically Scottish words and phrases, such as *ye ken* (you know) or *the noo* (now).

Parliamo Glasgow

In the 1970s, exuberant Scots-speaking comedian Stanley Baxter shot to international fame with a series of television broadcasts: *Parliamo Glasgow*.

Gently mocking an earnest BBC educational programme, *Parliamo Italiano* (Let's Speak Italian), the series developed from sketches first performed at Glasgow's famous Citizens Theatre. Straight-faced, Baxter posed as a university teacher explaining the mysteries of the Glasgow dialect of Scots to his viewers and listeners.

Baxter's most famous examples of Glasgow 'patter' made fun of the Glasgow habit of running several words together. They included **sanoffy**, as in *Sanoffy raw day* (It's an awfully cold and damp day), and **Zattafacmac?** (Is that indeed so, my fellow citizen?).

To which we might add **Itzarairterr**: Jolly good show!

Strange but true

In 2010, a London translation agency advertised – in the *Glasgow Herald*, where else? – for the world's first interpreter of Glaswegian. The agency wished to recruit someone willing and able to assist professional and business visitors to the city. The job vacancy attracted 480 applicants.

Say it this way: Weegie

Just a few examples of typical Glasgow sounds:

aff	off	*ra*	the
alang	along	*rat*	that
aun	on	*rye-it*	right
caur	car	*staun*	stand
drap	drop	*stoap*	stop
fillum	film	*waant*	want
hauf	half	*yin*	one

Edinburgh: radge or refined?

radge: wild, aggressive.

As Scotland's capital, and the centre of its government, legal business and (so it would like to think) culture, the splendid city of Edinburgh has developed two completely different ways of speaking. One is restrained and refined; think (in fiction and in film) Miss Jean Brodie. This educated, upper-middle-class Edinburgh dialect is traditionally linked with the exclusive residential district of Morningside (though it's also found in smart districts of other cities), and with practitioners in the Edinburgh lawcourts. On the whole, it makes use of grammar that would raise no eyebrows south of the Border, with just a smattering of Scottish vocabulary for objects or ideas that have no English equivalent.

Only a slight accent reveals that the Morningside speaker is Scottish. Along with other Scots, they roll their 'r's: *motherr*, *brotherr*. They also use a short, 'high' vowel sound in words such as *puir*, *fuid* and *guid*, a little like the French *u* in *mur*.

Scots legal language

absolvitur judgement whereby a court *assoilzies* a person

adjudication decision of a judge

advocate lawyer appearing in court; the equivalent of an English barrister or solicitor-advocate

advocate depute prosecutor working under the direction of the Lord Advocate

Advocate General chief Government advisor on Scots law

aliment maintenance of a spouse or child enforceable by law

assoilzie in criminal cases, to find not guilty. In civil cases, to find for the defendant.

delict negligent act causing loss

dispone transfer land

factor person who manages property or land on behalf of the owner

interdict court order made to prevent a particular action

interlocutor order made by a court during legal proceedings

Lord Advocate the senior Scottish law officer

Lord President top criminal judge in Scotland

Lords in Ordinary judges at the Court of Session (Scottish Supreme Court)

Missive of Sale written agreement setting out the terms of a sale

panel the accused in a local court case

policies the land and gardens surrounding a house

precognition preliminary statement by a witness

procurator fiscal public prosecutor and equivalent of the English coroner

pursuer plaintiff

Register of Sasines register of titles to land in Scotland

respondent defendant in a civil law case

sheriff judge in a local court

timeous within the time-period allowed by law

wrongous wrongful

Not proven

As well as finding an accused person guilty or not guilty, certain Scottish courts can also hand down a verdict of 'not proven'. This has been described by some as proof that Scots justice is fair and reasonable; others say that it means 'We know you're guilty but we can't find the evidence!'

A word of warning

If you fail to appear before a Scottish court, your presence will, of course, be missed – and you'll probably be punished. But, if you are a Scots speaker, you will also **miss yourself** there. In the same way, you might miss yourself (be absent) from work, or miss yourself from (decide not to go to) a party.

'Pure dead brilliant'

At the other end of the social spectrum, Edinburgh has some of Scotland's most spectacular street speech – and catchphrases. Several, like 'pure dead brilliant', come from Scottish television shows. Other Edinburgh dialect words have their origins in the Roma language, traditionally spoken by travelling people in southern Scotland. In recent years, these have found wider fame in novels and films such as Irvine Welsh's best-seller, *Trainspotting*.

Streetwise words

*Asterisked words are of Roma origin.

bampot mad; idiot. *'Shottie, ya bam!'*: Look out, you fool!

barry* very good

chanking very cold

cheesing very happy (from the habit of saying 'cheese' when being photographed)

Scottish Words

chorrie steal

chum accompany

deek* look

doosh hit, punch

foostie foul, stale

gadgie* man, boy

lowie money

manishee* girl

nash* hurry

pal* brother

pannie* river

shan* unfair

swedge fight

swind good, sound

tan take, get

wonga money (etymology unknown)

Soft and steady

Edinburgh everyday speech often uses neat combinations of auxiliary verbs that just aren't possible in English: *I used tae could do that!* ('I used to be able to do that'). It includes rhyming slang: *He's potted heid* for 'He's dead.' And (think Sean Connery!) it's spoken in a level accent that softens words containing the letters *tr* or *thr* – 'tree', for instance, may sound like *chtree*. In contrast with Glasgow speech, words such as 'barrow' (Glasgow: *barra*) are pronounced *barrae*. Edinburgh speakers are also likely to say *whae* (who), *yae* (one) and *twae* (two).

Potted heid, in case you were wondering, is a traditional Scottish delicacy involving a sheep's head.

J, J, J

Further north and east, the city of Dundee was traditionally famous for three industries: Jute, Jam and Journalism. All have left a lasting mark on the language. Without a certain Mrs Keiller at the end of the 18th century, the world today might not identify the word *marmalade* with orange jam; without publishers D. C. Thomson and Co, children throughout the UK might never have read a comic named *The Beezer* (a Dundee word that means 'excellent' or 'jolly good'). Many other Dundee words have their origins in the jute industry, which attracted immigrants to the city from Scotland, Ireland and South Asia during the 19th and early 20th centuries. Naturally, these new Dundonians brought some of their own words with them.

My heart wi' joy may up
be heized,
Or doon wi' sorrow worn,
But, Oh, it never can forget
The toon where I was born.

Robert Nicoll, 1814–1837. Nicoll, born in the village of Tullibardane, Perthshire, writes about Dundee as if it were his home town.

heize: lift; also, to hurry.

Speak Dundee

barkit very dirty

bummer jute-factory siren, used to call mill-
hands to work

fleg fright

gansey pullover

plenny pavement

plettie shared landing or lobby in front of a
tenement

rovies shoes made of jute, worn by women
factory workers

shorer swimming pool

The Dundee accent is famous for replacing the
sound *ai* (as in English 'I' or 'sky') with *eh*: *Eh wud
lehk a peh and a pehnt*. It also features distinctive
vowel-sounds: *whit* (what), *hoo* (how) and *whan*
(when). Like their neighbours in Fife, Dundee
people speak with a rising and falling intonation –
almost musical, some say!

Dialect stops dementia?

In 2010, experts at Abertay University in Dundee launched a study to investigate whether speaking the local dialect might help Dundee people over 60 to stave off dementia. They aim to test the theory that learning more than one language helps keep everyone 'mentally fit'.

Doric on the Don

After Glesga patter and Edinburgh's Morningside, the dialect spoken in and around Aberdeen, on the banks of the River Don, is probably the most easily recognised variety of Scots. Nicknamed 'Doric' (ancient Greek for 'rustic' or 'countrified') by an 18th-century scholar, Aberdeen Scots contains many words not used elsewhere in Scotland.

Distinctive Doric

aathing anything

bosie cuddle

bydand steadfast

craiter creature

dirdum upheaval, uproar

dubby muddy

Fit like? How's things?

forfauchan exhausted

gangrel a tramp

hellach noisy, awkward, defiant

plat piece of land

pucklie small quantity

sotter mess

swicking cheating

trig active

whilk which

'Furryboots'

The most striking feature of Doric pronunciation is the use of the sound 'f' for 'wh': *fit* (what), *faar* (where), *fan* (when) and even *fusky* (whisky). This way of speaking has led to Aberdeen being nicknamed the *furryboots* (whereabouts) city. In Aberdeen you will also hear *een* (one), *meen* (moon), *gweed* (good) and *nae* (no). Even more surprising to outsiders, perhaps, is that in a town where North Sea trawling was once the most important industry, the catch of 'silver darlings' (herring) is usually known as *fush* (fish).

Doric Festival

There is even a Doric Festival, described as:

> A twa wikk lang splore of the tung, sangs, music and traditions o oor byous Doric culture.
>
>   http://www.thedoricfestival.com/

splore: celebration; byous: extraordinary.

Still Scandinavian?

The far northern islands of Scotland, collectively known as Orkney and Shetland, were not part of the Scottish kingdom until 1468, when Scottish King James III married Princess Margaret of Denmark. Before then, and for many centuries afterwards, the local people communicated in Norn – a language based on Old Norse, as spoken by the Vikings. After around 1800, as contacts between Orkney, Shetland and the rest of Scotland increased, Norn almost disappeared. Most local people began to speak Scots, but with a strongly Norn flavour. Just a few pure Norn words survived, such as *speir* (ask) or *felkyo* (witch).

A splendid voice for telling stories in ...

Orkney poet Edwin Muir (1887–1959)
on the language of his homeland

Orkney

beer whine	**hosst** cough
blide happy	**nave** handful
fire throw	**peedie** small
gavse eat hungrily	**sprett** split

Shetland

anyatwark contrary	**perskeet** prim and proper
baffel struggle	
daffik bucket	**shoormal** highwater's edge
flan gust of wind	**voe** sea-inlet
gaa-bursen out of breath; exhausted	**yasp** lively

Who are you?

In Orkney and Shetland, the Scots (and English) words 'you' and 'yours' are usually replaced by *thu* or *ðu* and *thee* or *ðee* when referring to only one person:

Hoo are thu? (Orkney: 'How are you?')
Is ðu heard? (Shetland: 'Have you heard?'; in
   Shetland, the verb 'to be' is often used in place of
   'to have')
Take thee tea (Orkney: 'Drink your tea')
I hear ðee (Shetland: 'That sounds unlikely').

In Orkney, *whar* can mean both 'who' and 'where'. In Shetland, *wir* means 'our'. Also in Shetland, inanimate objects may be spoken of as if they are male or female: *He jost lowsed* ('It started to pour with rain'); *He's him a ðay* ('It's a bad day').

Traces of the islands' Viking past can still be heard in the local accents. Spoken Shetland sounds rather like Norwegian, with emphasis placed towards the end of a sentence, followed by a rising tone. Orkney is similar, but with a more up-and-down pitch; some people think it sounds rather like Welsh.

Scots or not?

Strange but true: some of the strongest supporters of the Scots language don't live in Scotland at all. Their homes are in Ireland, mostly in Ulster, in the north. Many are descended from Lowland Scottish families who were encouraged to settle in Northern Ireland during the 17th century. Who sent them there? The Protestant King James VI of Scotland/James I of England, together with wealthy Scottish and English 'undertakers' (investors). They wanted to settle the province with loyal Protestant subjects, after many years of fighting between English rulers and local Gaelic-speaking, Roman Catholic, Irish chiefs and their followers.

As well as these 'planted' Scots, from earliest times, many Scottish people travelled to work or trade in Ireland, and many Scottish sailors regularly visited Irish ports. Some of these visitors eventually settled permanently in Ireland. They brought their own Scots language (in Ireland, sometimes called 'Ullans') – and their own Scots literary traditions, especially Kailyard stories (see pages 73–74). Until the mid-20th century, Scots-speaking Northern Irish writers also wrote many humorous, folksy, country-life tales of their own.

For centuries, the whole island of Ireland was a scene of tragic conflict between rival communities, religions, political parties and would-be rulers. Even today, although peace has largely been restored, outward signs of heritage and identity, such as language, can still cause controversy. For example, there was opposition when the Ulster-Scots Language Society was formed in 1992, with the aim of 'protecting and promoting' the version of Scots spoken in Ulster. Although Ulster Scots has since been recognised as a Minority Language by the British Government (1999) and the European Community, critics still accuse it of being an 'artificial dialect'. They argue that 'real' Scots is no longer spoken in Ulster and that today's 'so-called' Ulster Scots is inaccurate, unhistorical, inauthentic and incomprehensible. On the other hand, almost 30% of Ulster inhabitants claim to speak it.

The Hamely Tongue*

Ulster Scots vocabulary is similar to the everyday Scots spoken in Edinburgh and the Scots Central Region. But there are some words now mostly confined to the province, such as:

answer fit or suit

culchie country person

danner walk

dull noose or snare

duncher cap

dyach naughty child

fornenst opposite, beside

gnuk steal

keen lament

nyitter complain

styaghey unappetising food

swaddy fat

thaveless incompetent

weefla (= wee fellow) boy

Unmissable

cat-melodeon (say: *kat-meh-LOW-ðjin*) awful din

* *title of a book (2006) by novelist and expert on Ulster Scots, James Fenton.*

Irish Gaelic influence

you or **yeh** (singular), **yous** or **youson** (plural)

I am: yes; **I am not**: no

It is: yes; **It is not**: no

Where Scots-Irish differs most from mainland and island Scots is in pronunciation. Some Scots-Irish speakers sound similar to mainland Scots, but others speak with a Northern Irish accent. Here are just a few examples:

A for I, as in *A cudnae see.*
cud, wud could, would (as in English *bud*)
fud found
pawed pod
beg bag
de-ays days
wet what
fer for
flure floor
kanl candle
owl old
Trilled *rrr* as in mainland Scots
ch as in mainland Scots 'loch'.

66

Sic as ye gie, sic wull ye get.

Traditional Scottish saying

sic: such; gie: give.

99

CHAPTER SIX

KITH AND KIN

Scots and English! How close? How distant? It's probably not very helpful – although true – to say that the two languages sometimes seem very similar to each other, and sometimes far apart. In this chapter we will look at a few Scots words and phrases that have travelled south to become part of regular everyday English, and at others which sound the same but have entirely different meanings on opposite sides of the Border.

We will also look at just a few of the other ways in which Scots and English are different. As well as having their own separate, distinctive vocabulary and pronunciation, Scots also use their own special grammar, syntax and idioms. And who has not heard of Scots exclamations or interjections such as *och* or *hoots, mon*? Or wondered why Scots-speakers say *no* or *nae* when often they mean 'yes'?

It's a borrow...

As the old Scots saying has it:

A borrow sudd gang lauchin hame.

A borrower should go laughing home (is very fortunate).

On the following few pages, you can see some Scots words and phrases used in English, with their original meanings.

Scots into English

blackmail originally, violent threats made by Scots Border *reivers* (raiders).

caddy The Scots word once meant 'army cadet' or 'rough young lad'. Now golf gives it another meaning.

clan a word of Gaelic origin (*clann*: children), borrowed first by the Scots and then by the English. When describing a group of people considered by others to be 'clannish' (not a Scots word), a Scots speaker might say that they are **aw ae oo**: all the same.

cosy It means 'warm and comfortable' in Scots, too, but also a sheltered place – and a woolly scarf.

cuddle possibly derived from Scots *couthie* (see page 85) or from a Dutch word, *kudden* (gather together).

eerie supernaturally scared, or scary. *Eerie* can describe either the feeling, or the cause of it. A word that had disappeared from English by around 1500, and had to be borrowed back again.

> For oh! the North's an eerie land…

Scots poet Violet Jacob,
'Northern Lights', 1927

firth a Viking word for a wide sea-inlet.

glamour an ancient Scottish word meaning 'magic' or 'enchantment'.

> Sae soon as they saw her weel-far'd face
> They cast a glamour o'er her…

From 'Johnny Fa and Earl Cassil's Lady',
a ballad about a noblewoman who runs
away with the gypsies (Roma people),
first written down around 1750

weel-far'd: lovely

heather the moorland plant which turns Scottish hills deep purple in late summer.
That'll no set the heather alicht: that's nothing to get excited about.

lad, lass in Scots, can also mean 'sweetheart':

> Gin a body meet a body
> Comin through the rye,
> Gin a body kiss a body
> Need a body cry?

> *Chorus:*

> Ilka lassie has a laddie;
> Nane, they say, hae I,
> Yet a' the lads they smile at me
> When comin' through the rye.

> Traditional song, often attributed
> (incorrectly) to Robert Burns

gin (pronounce with a hard g): when; a body: a person; rye: fields of growing rye; ilka: each.

link/links for Scots-speakers, a word with multiple meanings: the sandy, windswept, seaside place where games of golf are played, but also a lock of hair, a section of a chain, a joint in the body, a string of sausages, entwined arms – and a verb meaning to leap, act briskly, run away fast. *Pit a link in one's tail*: be deceitful.

plaid *not* a chequered pattern, not tartan, but any length of closely woven woollen cloth worn as a cloak or shawl. Striped and chequered plaids were popular and so – to outsiders – the name of the pattern became the name of the garment as well. *Cauking the claith afore the wab be in the luim:* counting your chickens before they are hatched (*cauking: washing or cleaning with chalk; claith: cloth; wab: web, threads; luim: loom*).

pony from *pownie*, a horse for riding (rather than for pulling carts or ploughing); also a carpenter's saw-horse.

raid an attack made on horseback. A word made popular in England by the novels of Sir Walter Scott (1771–1832). Related to English *ride*.

rampage a mixture of the old Scots word for a disturbance, *ram* or *rammy*, with the English word *rage*. A synonym is **rin wuid** (run mad).

scone a Dutch word, *schoonbrot* (fine bread), before it was Scots.

tweed thick, hairy woollen cloth with a **tweel** (diagonal) weave, often incorporating two or more subtly blended colours. It was once claimed that the name *tweed* came from the misreading of the word *tweel*, but experts now say that it came from the Scots **tweeled** (twisted), which describes the way that the cloth is woven. A related word is **tweedle**, 'twist together': *Staup tweedlin yer thoums!*

whisky As most lovers of the 'amber nectar' know, the name comes from two Gaelic words: *uisge beatha* (water of life). In the 19th century, after factory-made spirits became widely available throughout the Scottish Lowlands, Scots speakers called the drink at first *usquebae* and then, more simply, *whisky*.

wraith the Scots word for 'ghost' or 'spirit', of unknown origin.

> By this the storm grew loud apace,
> The water-wraith was shrieking;
> And in the face of heaven each face
> Grew dark as they were speaking.

From 'Lord Ullin's Daughter', by Glasgow-born Thomas Campbell (1777–1844)

False friends

That's what linguists call words which look the same but have different meanings in different languages. Here are just a few which might confuse non-Scots speakers:

away, awa often substitutes for the verb 'to go': *I'm away to my bed.*

body person. *There's a body in the bath!* But no need to call the police – in Scots that just means that someone is getting clean or enjoying a leisurely soak.

bunnet or **bonnet** headgear for men. Includes anything from a Rastafarian tam to a traditional tweed cap or something high-tech worn by mountaineers. Not, however, a pretty hat made of straw, lace and ribbons from a Jane Austen novel; in Scots, the little lace bonnet favoured by historical heroines is called a **mutch**.

cry call. *Oor dug's cry'd 'Spot'.*

depute deputy. As in **shirra-depute** (deputy sheriff).

fair rather, or, sometimes, very. *She was fair ramfeezled* (confused, puzzled).

gallows braces, to hold the trousers up. An old-fashioned name for an old-fashioned garment, but still used (and worn) by some men north of the Border.

grannie a metal cap or lid, usually revolving, fitted to the top of a chimneypot to reduce the risk of sudden downdraughts or generally to regulate the flow of air. Also, of course, a grandmother:

> Ye cannae push yer grannie aff a bus!
> Ye cannae push yer grannie aff a bus!
>   O ye cannae push yer grannie,
>   'Cos she's yer mammie's mammie,
> No, ye cannae push yer grannie aff a bus!

> Children's song made famous by Glaswegian folksingers Robin Hall and Jimmie MacGregor

greet cry. *She was greetin sair* (bitterly). **Greetie-gowlie**: child who cries all the time; **greetin-meetin**: a farewell.

haud (hold) keep, continue. *Haud ye merry!*:

Keep cheerful! *How are ye hauden?*: Are you keeping well?

hen dear (to a woman or girl). *Gie us a kiss, ma bonnie wee hen!* But *Like a hen on a hot girdle* (griddle): very restless; impatient.

hill mountain. Outdoor Scots enjoy 'a day in the hills' or 'hill-walking', however steep the slope or high the peak.

lair burial plot

loan strip of grassland; grassy pathway. In 1820, the *Scots Magazine* reported that villagers in Teviotdale claimed to see the Devil regularly, on a Saturday evening, taking a walk along the loan.

mains Nothing electrical, but the traditional term for a big home farm. Still the name of many hamlets and farmhouses in Lowland Scotland.

messages Shopping, usually for food. *Ah jist stepped oot [walked out, went] for my messages.*

mind remember. But NB in Scots, to forget can be to **disremember**.

outwith beyond, outside. *He stays outwith the city. It is outwith my powers to help you.* Similarly, Scots often say **inwith** (inside, within) and **inweys** (inwards).

pudding sausage. As in *black pudding* (made with blood), *white pudding* (made with oatmeal, fat and onions) or even *fruit pudding* (made with oatmeal, fat and currants). All are sliced, fried and served for breakfast. Black pudding can be deep-fried in batter and served with chips, to make a *black-pudding supper* (see page 94).

retiral can mean either 'retirement' or 'retiring' (as in 'retiring collection').

shabby in poor health – so in Scots you can be smart and shabby at the same time.

slogan originally a battle cry or secret password used among warriors. From the Gaelic, but adopted into Scots.

stance the place where you catch a bus. *The next bus for Kelvingrove leaves from stance no. 10.* In public notices, some bus companies use the word *standees* to denote standing passengers. A Glasgow friend of the author claims also to have seen the word *settees* used as a synonym for seated passengers, but she suspects that he may be trying to make her *hunt the gowk* (see page 114).

stand a set of bagpipes

take or **tak** consume. *Will ye no take a wee dram, Hamish?* Also, to suffer from an illness: *He takes the depression. She's taken the measles.*

tryst a cattle-market; also an agreement or meeting – but not, as in English, a romantic lovers' rendezvous. Between around 1600 and 1850, hundreds of thousands of prime black beef cattle were walked south from the Highlands and western islands to be sold at Lowland trysts. The largest was at Falkirk.

uplift collect, take away. *Has the postie uplifted the mail, the day?*: Has the postman collected today's letters?

widdle struggle; tremble. Yes, really.

Ways of saying

In a little book like this, there is no space to describe the rules of Scots grammar or syntax – that is, the way words are shaped and sentences arranged to show a speaker's meaning. But, like any other proper language, Scots does have them. Here are just a few examples of how Scots uses words in its own very special way. (English equivalents are given in brackets.)

Articles

The mither's awfu wabbit the day. ('the' for 'my')

He's a terrible man for the lassies! (meaning 'lassies in general')

They've gone to the fishing. (gone fishing)

Robert the Bruce The great Scots hero's surname is rarely used without the definite article.

The chookie laid a egg. (*a*, not *an*, before a vowel)

'Luve is ane fervent fire…' (*an* before a consonant)

from Alexander Scott (1520–1590),
'A Rondel of Love'

Singular and plural

The wean's got bonnie blue een. (eyes)

a braw pair o shune (shoes)

He walked a hunder mile. (singular for plural)

That's twa pund, please. (singular for plural)

Prepositions

She has five tae (or of) a family. (a family of five)

He's marrit on a French lassie. ('on' for 'to')

Will ye tak a wee drap parritch tae your breakfast?'
  ('of' understood; 'tae' for 'for')

He's an engineer to trade. (by)

Ah'm waitin on the bus frae Dundee. (for)

The besom's fawen oot on a her neebors. (with)

Pronouns

That's me finished. (I've finished.)

Yon's the man that's dug worrit the yowes. (whose)

'Are you happy?' 'I am that.' ('Yes, I am.')

Verb forms

Ah'm a Scotsman, amn't I? English uses *aren't* as
the negative of *am*; the Scots form is much more
logical.

Ah telt him! (told) In Scots the past tense keeps
the same vowel as the present tense.

She kent weel the road to the shore. (knew; past tense
of *ken*)

They says he's a sair clype. (say)

Ma brakes have went. (have gone)

*Ah wud hav went to the toon, but ah dinnae hav ony
petrol.* (would have gone)

Thaim fush is bowfin. Aw of thaim's rotten. ('is' for
'are')

*They wis all but [outside] the kirk when it blowstered
[rained heavily].* ('wis' for 'were')

I used tae could dance the Hieland Fling. (used to be
able to)

He wouldna could dae that. (wouldn't be able to)

Ah'm away hame. ('away' substitutes for the verb 'going')

The bairns wants tae go soomin [swimming], an the wind sae snell. (although the wind is so bitter)

Conjunctions

She's better nor she's bonnie. (than)

Adverbs

She's awfu bonnie. (awfully, very)

That's a real good film. (really)

Some distinctive Scots adverbs are quite unrelated to their English equivalents:

Aiblins ye'll feel better the morrow. (Perhaps)

> *When merry Yule-day comes, I trow,*
> *You'll scantlins find a hungry mou;* (scarcely)

> From Robert Fergusson (1750–1774),
> 'The Daft-Days'

Ye'll see coffee shops awgates in Edinbroo. (everywhere)

Diminutives

Scots vocabulary is fond of diminutives (word-endings such as *-ie* that indicate smallness or endearment). Sometimes a whole series of them may be piled up.

She's a nebbie [sharp-tongued] wee wifie.

The scaffie's doon the midden.

Thir rhodies [rhododendron bushes, a landscape pest in parts of Scotland] are killin the birks [birch trees].

Wee usually means 'very small' or 'very weak', but sometimes, for emphasis, it can mean just the opposite:

'In the name of the wee man!' Damn! (literally, 'For the sake of the Devil')

Negatives

Double negatives – often considered objectionable in English – are perfectly acceptable in Scots:

A'm no gaun tae tell ye naething I'm not going to tell you anything.

She niver wears nae gluves She never wears gloves.

nevernane (*never + nae + ane*) no-one

Negative tags may be added to a question, to show that the speaker expects a positive reply:

Jeannie speaks the Gaelic, does she no?

It's a braw day, eh no?

Some positive questions can sound negative:

Will ye no step ben the hoose?

Negative structures in Scots may differ subtly from the English form:

'Ah've nivver met her.' 'Och! Have ye not?' (Haven't you?)

He cannae come oot, the noo. He's no taen his tea. (He hasn't had)

And, just when we think we see a nice neat pattern:

Double positives can have a negative meaning:

Aye, right? (Of course not!)

Survivals

Speakers of medieval or Tudor English would have no difficulty in understanding these phrases which are still current in Scots:

Lief is me on (I am pleased with)

I was as lief (I would rather)

Spelling Scots

Astonishingly, even in the 21st century, there is no standard way of spelling Scots words. And that's official! According to a leading Scottish Government educational agency, we should regard this as an opportunity, not a failure:

> ... having no standard allows Scots writers great freedom.

http://ltscotland.org.uk/

Some others are not so sure. They contrast this *blithe* informality with the requirements of the Scottish National Curriculum for the English language, which insist that students write 'legibly and with accurate spelling and punctuation'. They ask, 'Why not treat Scots equally?'

The answer may well lie *fankled* (entangled) in the intricacies of Scottish dialect. With so many different local variations to choose from, which Scottish region's words would be considered the most correct – and what about those spoken elsewhere?

Letters and sounds

Scottish spelling preserves the traces of a letter that has long since disappeared from modern English, the Old English *yogh* (ȝ), pronounced like modern *y*. Until around 1700, Scots words such as 'year' were spelt with ȝ. It can still be seen today, but modernised as *z*, for example in the Scottish surname Menzies (pronounced 'Ming-gyiz').

> A lively young damsel named Menzies
> Inquired: 'Do you know what this thenzies?'
>   Her aunt, with a gasp,
>   Replied: 'It's a wasp,
> And you're holding the end where the stenzies.'

© John Menzies plc; used with permission

Scottish pronunciation also retains a number of Old English sounds that have been dropped by modern English speakers, for example:

• *ch* as in *loch*, *nicht* corresponds to English *gh*, which is usually no longer pronounced.

• Most Scots speakers still make a clear distinction between the *wh*-sound of *which* (now rarely heard in English) and the *w*-sound of *witch*. The *wh*-sound in Scots is sometimes spelt *quh* or *qwh*, especially in proper names such as Farquhar.

• *Sch* as in *schaw* (to show; also the stalks of root crops) represents a sound quite distinct from English *show*.

• *Wr* is now pronounced *vr* in northeast Scots, as in *vrang* (wrong); in English, a *w* in this position is no longer pronounced.

Books of words

The fact that there is still no universal standard for Scots spelling is not the fault of dedicated compilers of dictionaries. After Boswell's half-forgotten attempt (see page 60), the first completed dictionary of Scots words, by John Jamieson, appeared in 1808. In the 20th century, it took over 40 years of painstaking research to compile the 10-volume *Scottish National Dictionary*, which was finally completed in 1976. The 12 volumes of the historical *Dictionary of the Older Scottish Tongue* took even longer to put together, from 1931 to 2002. Marvellously, both works are now available online, for free.

In 1983, another cultural landmark appeared in the shape of William Lorimer's translation of the New Testament into Scots. Lorimer's style is lively, vivid, flowing: his text was hailed as a fine work of literature as well as an aid to devotion. It became a bestseller.

In 2011, research staff of the SWAP (Scottish Words and Place-names) project invited Scots-speakers to help keep national language collections right up to date by contributing current Scots words to a new online dictionary. The project concluded in November 2011, but words can still be submitted using the input forms on the website.

"

'Scots is fantastically expressive. Not knowing it is a loss, a lack.'

Scots language campaigner J. Derrick McClure,
quoted in *The Guardian*, 20 May 2011

"

CHAPTER SEVEN

A' OOR AIN

All our own.

I t is sometimes said that you can never hope to understand a people or their culture unless you can speak their language. If that is true, then it's no wonder that the English and the Scots so often criticise each other – even if only through force of habit, rather than for real. It's also not surprising that, from time to time, supporters of the Scots language get very worried. If, as they fear, Scots is becoming less widely spoken, will Scots men, women and children forget their culture, their identity?

Changing times

In the early 21st century, experts studying street language in Edinburgh made a rather shocking discovery: some young Scottish people were no longer saying typical Scots words in a typically Scottish way. In particular, they were losing the guttural *ch* in words such as *loch*. Around the same time, further experts found that Glasgow neds (see page 121) also favoured certain non-Scottish ways of speaking, for example, saying *glahss* instead of *glass*.

What's going on? Is modern Scottish speech being influenced from south of the Border or across the Atlantic by rock and rap, movies and TV, Cockney slang or Estuary English? Perhaps, just a little bit. But, as the experts warned, young people have always found ways of being different from their elders. So who knows? Today's young people may all be talking braid Scots like their ancestors by the time they reach 40 years old.

'There's no ane of them to mend anither'

So far, in this book, we have indulged – just a bit – in the traditional 'Scots cringe'. We have blamed all kinds of 'others' – kings, nobles, the Kirk, the English – for the slow decline of the Scots language. However, as the Scots proverb above makes clear (it means 'They're both as bad as each other'), Scottish people themselves must also take their fair share of the blame.

In the 19th century, many socially ambitious Scottish men and women followed the example of earlier Edinburgh elites, and rejected Scots. As Robert Ford, a keen observer of Scottish popular culture, complained in 1891:

> The snobbish element among the great middle class, ever prone to imitate their 'betters', affect not to understand it [Scots]...a portion of the semi-educated working population...speak Scotch only in their working clothes.

At the same time, with the aid of the *tawse* (leather strap) and in the name of helping children to get 'a good education', Scottish teachers banned Scots words from being spoken, written or read in Scottish schools. They forbade Gaelic, also. They declared that Scots was slang, bad English, inferior. Gaelic was simply barbarous.

Scots on the air

From 1923, Scottish accents, and a very great deal of traditional Scottish dance music, were heard on the airwaves after BBC radio began broadcasting to Scotland, and Scottish broadcasters began contributing their own programmes to the network. A 'hamely' Scottish comedy series, *The McFlannels* (I am not making this up), did feature some Scots words, but most early Scottish BBC staff spoke Standard Scottish English (SSE), just like other well-educated middle-class Scots from Edinburgh and elsewhere.

The first TV broadcast to Scotland was in 1952: the funeral of King George VI, from London. The first TV programmes transmitted from Scotland, in the same year, were a prayer, a speech from the Lord Provost of Edinburgh (both in SSE) – and, yes, ten long minutes of Scottish dancing. Even BBC Controller Lord Reith (a Scotsman) thought they were boring.

In the decades that followed, there was improvement. There were educational TV programmes about Scots-language poets and writers, and even a major series on the history of Scots words and grammar. Scots speakers appeared on Scottish radio and TV – in everything from Andy Stewart's sterotype-stuffed *White Heather Club* to hard-hitting working-class comedies such as *Rab C. Nesbitt* (BBC Scotland, 1988–1999, revived 2010–2014). In 2011, a sad and shocking documentary series, *The Scheme*, featured Scots-speaking people with troubled lives in a deprived district of Kilmarnock. But, almost always, Scots was treated by media folk as a minority (or dead, or dangerous, or obscure) way of speaking.

There is still no mainstream Scots-language TV channel – though there has been a dedicated Gaelic radio channel since 1985, and Gaelic TV since 1996. Gaelic, spoken by fewer people than Scots, is more generously funded by broadcasters and others. A total of over £24 million was spent on Gaelic-related projects by the Scottish Government in 2010.

Words worth knowing

However, let's suppose – as the evidence in fact suggests – that non-Scots-speakers can happily get to know, love and understand Scotland and its people without learning to speak the Scots language. Even so, there are still a few Scots words and phrases that might be useful for anyone who wishes to get up close and personal with Scottish culture. Every Scots speaker will have their own favourites, but in 2007 *The Scotsman* newspaper published a list of the Best Scottish Words. We have met many of them already, but here they are, all together:

Top 10 Scots words

1. **bauchle** originally, an old, worn-out shoe; now used to describe an unpleasant, scruffy person.

2. **blether** talk, chatter

3. **dreich** bleak, grim, dreary

4. **fankle** tangle

5. **gallus** cheeky, self-confident, mischievous

6. **mooch** a mixture of inquisitive and acquisitive

7. **pockle** to pocket (take away, wrap up)

8. **slitter** something spilled, a mess

9. **wabbit** weak and feeble

10. **wheesht** hush, shut up

They all sound wonderful – just say them out loud – and perhaps that is why they were chosen. But what else do they tell us about Scotland, the land and its people?

We nivver dee'd o winter yet

We'll survive!

In spite of over a hundred years of neglect, disapproval and outright disparagement, the Scots language today seems to be recovering, not dying. In the first-ever Scottish Government survey of Scots, made in 2010, 85% of the people questioned said that they spoke the language. At the same time, 67% said that they also considered it 'integral to Scotland's culture, heritage and local identities'.

A few enthusiasts perhaps take their support for Scots a little too far (see opposite), but the majority of Scottish people are pleased and proud to know the language. They may speak it all the time – particularly if they live in the far northeast and the islands – or may use only a few Scots words for which there is no easy English translation. Their communications are also flexible. As linguists say, they 'code-shift' between Scots and English as circumstances demand, depending on their mood, the occasion or the company.

You say 'potato' – I say 'tattie'!

In 2009, Scottish Nationalist MSP Brian Wilson excited controversy – and not a little ridicule – by writing to supermarkets in Scotland demanding that they use Scots to label fruit and vegetables.

The supermarkets rejected his request, claiming that Scots-speaking purchasers could clearly see and identify all items displayed for sale, and that labels in more than one language would confuse tourists.

Mr Wilson was making a Nationalist point – and was absolutely right to recognise that the use (or otherwise) of the Scots language is a deeply political matter. In the same year that he launched his bid to give vegetables their Scots names, Scottish Minister of Culture Linda Fabiani, also from the SNP, felt it necessary to declare: 'Scots is a living language to be cherished and supported.'

Today, Scots-speaking MSPs can even take the oath on joining Parliament in Scots:

I depone aat I wull be leal and bear aefauld
alleadgance tae her Majesty Queen Elizabeth,
her airs and ony fa come aifter her, anent the
law. Sae help me God.

*depone: swear, testify; leal: loyal; aefauld: single,
undivided (literally 'onefold'); anent: in accordance with.*

If anyone is, by now, wondering why supporters
of Scots feel the need to protest quite so much,
they have only to turn to the leading liberal,
progressive newspaper in the UK:

> Scotland won't be the first country to emphasise
> (exaggerate?) its linguistic separateness as a
> precursor to independence.

The Guardian, 20 May 2011

There is only one possible rejoinder: 'Awa and bile
yer heid!'

Fast forward

Scots has been 'dying' since around 1700 – but it's not gone yet! And today, in many ways, the future is looking bright for the next generation of Scots speakers. Pioneering publishers such as Itchy Coo, founded in 2002, produce 'braw books for bairns o aw ages', only in Scots. Scottish Government policies encourage the reading, writing and singing of Scots in schools. Poets, playwrights, novelists and many more use their creative powers to compose exciting works in the Scots tongue, for adults and for younger readers.

Two of the children's classics translated for Itchy Coo:

The Hoose at Pooh's Neuk by A. A. Milne

neuk: corner.

The Sleekit Mr Tod by Roald Dahl

sleekit (here): cunning, clever, crafty; tod: fox.

'Of a' the airts...'

(See page 106)

Modern media also spread the word, in all possible senses. You can find Scots out there in cyberspace, from friendly www.scuilwab.org.uk – launched in 2010 with the slogan 'leuk efter yer leid [language]' – to sharp and shocking collections of Scots city slang that would bring a blush to many a *primsie* (prim and proper), *douce* (mild, sedate, respectable) countenance. If you wish, online, you can read the Lord's Prayer in Norn (the Norse language that shaped the Scots spoken in Orkney and Shetland), or take part in a Scots chatroom live, or listen to Scotland's best actors reciting Robert Burns's incomparable love-songs.

http://www.orkneyjar.com/orkney/nornprayer.htm
http://www.scots-online.org/
http://www.bbc.co.uk/arts/robertburns/works/

And so, in all these ways and many more, Scots survives. It's a link to the past, and a reminder of Scotland's richly varied heritage. It's a political statement, supporting the Scotch claim to be the 'best small country in the world' and – at least for some Scots – pointing the way towards a fully independent future. Above all, Scots is a living language, full of wonderful words, from *shilpit* (thin) and *skellum* (rogue), *waukrife* (wakeful) and *wanchance* (risky) to *dirdum* (uproar), *ferlie* (marvel), *ramsh* (unpleasant), *intimmers* (innards) and *tirrivee* (excitement). Not forgetting *killywimple* (trill), *eechie-ochie* (either/or) and *heels-ower-gowrie* (head over heels), of course.

No wonder Scots is still spoken by Scottish men, women and children every day, everywhere – and, doubtless, whispered in their dreams.

> After all, the world's anthem of friendship, 'Auld Lang Syne', is composed in Scots.

The Scotsman, 12 March 2006

And what better tribute could any language hope for?

A Scots timeline

c.3000 BC – c.800 BC (experts do not agree) Celtic languages begin to be spoken in Scotland.

c.AD 600 First speakers of Anglo-Saxon arrive in Scotland, following earlier arrivals from Denmark and the northern Netherlands.

c.1300 Earliest recorded phrases in Scots: part of a poem about Scottish King Alexander III. Although the original text does not survive, a few lines are preserved as quotations in the work of later writers.

1340s Scribes write around 50 Scots glosses (explanatory notes) in the margins of an important Scottish legal document, the 1312 Charter of Scone.

1375 Oldest surviving complete work of literature in Scots: John Barbour's poem *The Brus* (Bruce). It is preserved in a copy made just over 100 years later.

1385 Oldest surviving document written in Scots: a writ (legal letter of instruction).

1386 Oldest surviving diplomatic use of Scots: the Billymire Truce, in which a Scottish nobleman negotiates a pause in Border wars with England.

c.1420 First known history in Scots: Andrew of Wyntoun, *Orygynale Cronykil*.

c.1420–1600 Makars (leading poets who write in Scots) are welcomed at the Scottish royal court.

c.1424 Scottish King James I writes *The Kings Quhair*.

1424–1707 Official records of the Scottish Parliament are kept in Scots.

1438 Oldest surviving romance (love-and-adventure story) in Scots, *The Buik of Alexander*.

1456 First known translation from French into Scots: Gilbert Hay's *Buke of the Law of Armys*.

c.1494 First known use of *Scottis* as a name for the Scots language, by Adam Loutfut.

1508 First known book printed in Scotland, by Chepman and Myllar of Edinburgh.

c.1530 First attempt to translate the New Testament into Scots, by Murdoch Nisbet.

1545 First known document in Scots issued in northern Ireland.

1560 Protestant Scottish Kirk breaks away from Roman Catholic Church, but retains English translation of the Bible and Psalms.

1584 Scottish King James VI publishes rules for poetry in Scots, composes poems himself, and encourages other Scots writers.

1603 James VI becomes James I of England. Moves royal court to England. Speaks and writes in English.

1649 King Charles I of Scotland and England dies; he is the last king to have spoken Scots.

1707 Scotland is united with England. Meetings of Scots Parliament are suspended for almost 300 years. Influential Scots move to London, the political centre of the new United Kingdom.

1707–1800 Scots speakers and people with Scottish accents are mocked by the English.

1724 Edinburgh poet Allan Ramsay publishes popular *Tea-Table Miscellany* in Scots. His works encourage madcap Scots poet Robert Fergusson (d. 1774).

1761 English elocution classes are held in Edinburgh.

1764 James Boswell plans a Scots dictionary. It is never completed, but some draft text survives.

1786 Robert Burns publishes *Poems, Chiefly in the Scottish Dialect.*

1808 John Jamieson publishes first complete *Etymological Dictionary of the Scottish Language.*

1814 Sir Walter Scott's first novel, *Waverley*, is set in Scotland and includes some Scots dialogue.

1845 Government Inspectors of Schools discourage the use of Scots.

1850–1900 Mass-circulation newspapers begin. Only a few articles are in Scots.

1872 Education Act effectively bans use of Scots in schools.

1873 James Murray publishes a pioneering scholarly study: *The Dialect of the Southern Counties of Scotland.*

c.1880–1910 Scottish writers of the 'Kailyard School' publish sentimental, nostalgic stories in Scots.

1922 Hugh MacDiarmid begins to publish poetry in Scots. Later, he campaigns for revival of 'Lallans' (a literary form of the Scots language).

1923 Radio broadcasting begins in Scotland; mostly in Standard Scottish English, although there are a few programmes in Scots.

1931–1976 *Scottish National Dictionary* compiled.

1931–2002 *Dictionary of the Older Scots Tongue* compiled.

1948 Scots poets meeting in Edinburgh try to introduce standard spelling and style for Scots.

1952 First TV broadcasts in Scotland; most are in English or Standard Scottish English.

1970 Association for Scottish Literary Studies founded.

1972 Lallans Society (now Scots Language Society) founded.

1983 W. Lorimer publishes New Testament in Scots.

1983 Annual anthology *New Writing Scotland* founded; it includes some works in Scots.

1985 Michael Munro's book *The Patter* raises awareness of Glasgow street language, which soon features in Scottish TV comedies, such as *Rab C. Nesbitt* (1988 onwards).

c.1990 onwards Leading Scottish writers, including Alastair Gray, James Kelman, Ian Rankin, Irvine Welsh and Alexander McCall Smith, use Scots words and phrases in their works.

1991 Scots language proposed as part of Scottish National Curriculum.

1996 Scottish National Party announces support for Scots language – the first political party to do so.

1998 Tha Boord o Ulster Scots/Ulster Scots Agency is set up to promote Scots language and culture in Northern Ireland.

1999 After a referendum and vote in favour of devolution (1997), the Scottish Parliament meets again, in Edinburgh.

2000 Members of the Scottish Parliament are allowed to take the oath of allegiance in Scots.

2001 UK Government ratifies European Charter for Minority Languages; this formally recognises Scots as a minority language.

2011 Question about knowledge of Scots is included in the Scottish Census.

2012 It is reported that previously unknown songs by Michael Jackson, with words by Robert Burns, will be donated to the Robert Burns Birthplace Museum.

2016 The Scottish Independence-supporting newspaper, The National, publishes an edition written partly in the Scots language.

General index

Index of Scots words